HOUGHTON MIFFLIN

California Science

Interactive Text

HOUGHTON MIFFLIN   BOSTON

Printed in the United States

ISBN 13: 978-0-547-00464-8
ISBN 10: 0-547-00464-8

18 19   0877   20 19 18

4500702586

Contents

Parts of Ecosystems 2

Interactions of Living Things 30

Energy in Ecosystems 56

Matter in Ecosystems 74

Rocks and Minerals 100

Rapid Changes on Earth 120

Slow Changes on Earth 138

Electricity 156

Magnetism and Electromagnets 176

Index 196

Credits 204

KWL

WHAT DO YOU KNOW?

List something that you know about each of these topics. You can also draw a picture to show what you know.

a. Nonliving parts of ecosystems _____

_____

b. Living parts of the ecosystems _____

_____

c. Land ecosystems _____

_____

d. Water ecosystems _____

_____

Parts of Ecosystems

Contents

1 What Are Nonliving Parts of Ecosystems?.. 4

2 What Are Living Parts of Ecosystems? ... 8

3 What Are Some Land Ecosystems? 14

4 What Are Some Water Ecosystems?..... 20

Glossary 25

WHAT DO YOU WANT TO KNOW?
What questions do you have about the nonliving and the living parts of ecosystems?

_____

_____

_____

_____

What questions do you have about different kinds of land ecosystems?

_____

_____

_____

_____

What questions do you have about different kinds of water ecosystems?

_____

_____

_____

_____

3

VOCABULARY

ecosystem All the living and nonliving things that interact in an area. *(noun)*

VOCABULARY SKILL: Prefix/Suffix

The prefix *eco-* means "house." How does knowing the meaning of the prefix *eco-* help you understand the meaning of the word *ecosystem*?

_____

_____

_____

_____

1 What Are Nonliving Parts of Ecosystems?

Things that do not need air, water, or food are nonliving things. Water, air, and sunlight are nonliving things. They help living things meet their needs.

Ecosystems and Nonliving Things

Look outside. You will see an ecosystem (EE koh sihs tuhm). An **ecosystem** has living and nonliving things. Water, air, soil, and light are nonliving things.

Living things need nonliving things. Most plants need soil to grow. They need sunlight to make food and keep warm. Some plants can only live where it is warm. Some grow better in shade. Shade protects living things from sunlight and heat.

nonliving things

3.a. Students know ecosystems can be described by their living and nonliving parts.

Nonliving things are different in different ecosystems. A forest and a polar area are both ecosystems. A polar area is cold and covered with ice. A forest and a polar area both have water, sunlight, soil, and air. But they act differently. In a polar area the water and ground freeze. Some plants and animals cannot live in this cold weather.

forest

polar area

1. (Circle) the ecosystem in which a penguin would live.

2. Study the forest ecosystem. List two nonliving things in this ecosystem.

   a. _____

   _____

   b. _____

   _____

5

3. Which nonliving part of a forest ecosystem do plants use to make food?

_____

I Wonder . . . What would happen to a forest ecosystem if suddenly there were no air?

_____

_____

_____

_____

6

Forest Ecosystem

LIGHT Most plants need light to make food.

AIR Plants and animals need air to live.

WATER A stream gives water to plants and animals.

SHADE Some plants grow well in the shade of trees.

SOIL Soil gives plants support and nutrients.

Different Ecosystems

Ecosystems have nonliving parts. Light, water, and soil are nonliving things. They help plants and animals meet their needs. A living thing can only live in a place where its needs are met.

Desert Ecosystem

It is very hot during the day in the desert. There is almost no rain. The soil is dry and has few nutrients. Desert plants and animals still find ways to meet their needs. Many animals only go out at night when it is cooler.

Polar Ecosystem

All the soil in a polar ecosystem has ice on it. It is very cold. There is little sunlight for half of the year. Only a few animals can live there. Their thick fur and fat keep them warm.

CLASSIFY

What conditions would you find in a polar ecosystem?

Summary The nonliving parts of an ecosystem determine which living things can live there. Use the chart to describe the nonliving parts of desert and polar ecosystems.

Nonliving Part	Desert Ecosystem	Polar Ecosystem
Temperature		
Soil		
Sunlight		

Classify What conditions would you find in a polar ecosystem?

Polar Ecosystem

7

VOCABULARY

community All of the organisms in an ecosystem. *(noun)*

energy The ability to cause change. *(noun)*

environment Everything that surrounds and affects an organism. *(noun)*

organism A living thing. *(noun)*

oxygen A gas most animals need to survive. *(noun)*

population All the members of one kind of plant or animal in a community. *(noun)*

reproduce To make more organisms of their own kind. *(verb)*

temperate zone An area of Earth where the temperature rarely gets very hot or very cold. *(noun)*

VOCABULARY SKILL: Word Phrases

The word *temperate* means "far from extreme." How does this definition help you understand the meaning of the phrase *temperate zone*?

_____

_____

2 # What Are Living Parts of Ecosystems?

Living things need nonliving things to meet their needs. Plants and animals meet their needs in their ecosystem.

Traits of Living Things

An **organism** (AWR guh nihz uhm) is a living thing. All organisms have needs. What does an organism need to live?

Energy You need energy (EHN ur jee) to move or breathe. **Energy** is what causes change. Plants use energy to make food. Animals get energy by eating. All organisms need energy.

Nutrients Organisms get energy from nutrients. Nutrients are parts of food and soil that give energy.

Air Air is made up of gases. One of them is **oxygen** (AHK sih juhn). Animals need oxygen to live. Plants give off oxygen.

Shelter A shelter is a place to live. It keeps an organism safe.

Water Living things are made of water. Most can only go a short time without it.

Bats find shelter in caves.

3.a. Students know ecosystems can be described by their living and nonliving parts.

How are a living bat and a toy animal different? The bat is alive and has life processes. A life process is something an organism does to live and reproduce (re pruh DOOS). Organisms **reproduce** by making more organisms.

Life Processes

Life Process		What It Means
take in nutrients		Organisms take in air, water, sunlight, and nutrients.
use energy		They get energy from nutrients in food.
grow		They use energy to grow.
react to ecosystem		They react to changes in their ecosystem.
give off waste		They give off oxygen and other gases.
reproduce		They make more young.

1. Look at the needs of living things listed on page 8. A cave is an example of one of these needs. Draw a box around that need. Where do bats meet this need?

_____

_____

2. Living things are different from the nonliving things you learned about in Lesson 1. Make an X in the table next to each process carried out by living or nonliving things. The first one has been done for you.

Process	Living Things	Nonliving Things
Take in nutrients	X	
Use energy		
Grow		
React to ecosystem		
Give off waste		
Reproduce		

3. Describe the temperature of an ecosystem found in a temperate zone.

_____

_____

I Wonder . . . Would you find a polar bear in a temperate zone? What do you think?

_____

_____

_____

Communities and Populations

Ecosystems are made up of all living and nonliving things. The forest shown here is an ecosystem. It is found in a temperate (TEHM pur iht) zone. A **temperate zone** is an ecosystem where it does not get very hot or very cold. A lot of organisms live in these ecosystems. The good weather lets many plants and animals meet their needs.

Deer rely on grasses and leaves for food.

An organism can only live in an environment (ehn VY ruhn muhnt) that meets its needs. An **environment** is all the things that affect an organism.

All of the organisms in an ecosystem make a **community** (kuh MYOO nih tee). In a community, there are different populations (pahp yuh LAY shunz). A **population** is all of one kind of plant or animal in an area. All of the moose in one area make up a population.

This is a moose in its environment.

4. An environment is all the things that affect an organism. List three things that affect the moose in its environment.

a. _____

b. _____

c. _____

5. How is a community different from a population?

_____

_____

_____

_____

6. Trees are living things in a forest ecosystem. How do warblers and beavers use trees to meet their need for shelter?

_____

_____

_____

_____

7. What type of plant grows best in the shaded area of a forest ecosystem?

_____

Forest Ecosystem

Warblers use trees for shelter.

Beavers use trees to build shelters.

Trillium plants grow best in the shade.

Conditions in Ecosystems

A terrarium is an example of an ecosystem. A terrarium is a small, closed place where plants and animals live. Different places in a terrarium meet different needs. In the picture, the rock and sticks under the lamp are hot and dry. But under the soil it is cool and wet. Ecosystems are also different. Organisms live where they can best meet their needs.

Model Ecosystem

Summary Organisms depend on nonliving things to meet their needs. They live in places where their needs are met. Use the chart to summarize how different parts of an ecosystem help living things meet their needs.

Part of Ecosystem	Need It Helps an Organism Meet
sunlight	_____
nutrients	_____
air and water	_____
shelter	_____

Cause and Effect Why must organisms meet their basic needs?

_____

_____

_____

CAUSE AND EFFECT

Why must organisms meet their basic needs?

13

VOCABULARY

chaparral An ecosystem with wet and mild winters and extremely hot and dry summers. *(noun)*

desert A dry ecosystem with sandy soil. *(noun)*

rainforest An ecosystem where it rains a lot. *(noun)*

taiga A fairly dry ecosystem with very cold, long winters and short, cool summers. *(noun)*

VOCABULARY SKILL: Compound Words

Some words are made up of two words. You can use the meanings of each word to discover the meaning of the compound word. *Rainforest* is a compound word. Write your own definitions of *rain* and *forest*.

rain: _____

forest: _____

How do these words help you understand what a rainforest is?

_____

---

3 What Are Some Land Ecosystems?

Plants and animals live in an ecosystem because of the nonliving things around it.

Tropical Rainforest

A **rainforest** (RAYN fawr ihst) is an ecosystem where it rains a lot. It is warm all year. Rainforests have a lot of life. Thousands of different plants and animals live there. These organisms like the sunlight, rain, and warm weather.

A tropical rainforest has different parts. A canopy is the area at the top of the tall trees. Birds, monkeys, and other animals make their home there. Other organisms live in the understory. The understory is the shady place under the tree tops. Some organisms live on the forest floor. It is shady.

Light, water, and shelter are different in all the sections of the tropical rainforest.

A rainforest is an ecosystem with a lot of rain.

Tropical Rainforest Ecosystem

CANOPY The top of the rainforest is the canopy. Tall trees use the sunlight to meet their needs. Many animals find food and shelter here.

UNDERSTORY Smaller trees and bushes live in the understory. It gets some sunlight.

FOREST FLOOR There is a lot of shelter, water, and shade on the forest floor.

1. Animals that live on the floor of the tropical rainforest use the trees and plants for food and shelter. Circle two organisms that live on the forest floor.

I Wonder . . . Smaller plants that live in the understory of a rainforest get some sunlight that filters through the rainforest's canopy. What would happen if the canopy of a rainforest blocked all the sunlight?

_____

_____

_____

_____

_____

2. List three characteristics of a desert ecosystem.

a. _____

b. _____

c. _____

3. Where are desert ecosystems found in the United States?

_____

_____

Desert

A **desert** (DEH zurt) is a dry ecosystem with sandy soil. In some deserts, it only rains once a year. Weather during the day is very hot. The soil has few nutrients.

There are deserts all over the world, including in the western United States.

All deserts have plenty of sunlight, very little rain, and few nutrients in the soil. But different organisms live in different deserts. These plants and animals are able to live in this environment. They find what they need to live. Organisms living in American deserts are not the same as organisms living in other deserts.

The desert is an ecosystem where plants and animals survive in harsh conditions.

4. Animals that live in deserts find what they need to live. Look at the picture of the desert. How might animals in this ecosystem survive hot daytime temperatures?

_____

_____

_____

_____

I Wonder . . . Deserts are dry places. Would you expect to find plants with thin leaves or with thick, waxy leaves in a desert? What do you think?

_____

_____

_____

17

5. A chaparral ecosystem has lots of fires. How do fires help some plants in these ecosystems?

_____

_____

_____

6. Trees found in the taiga stay green all year. These trees are called _____.

Chaparral

The American West is also home to some chaparral (shap ur AL) ecosystems. A **chaparral** has wet, mild winters but hot, dry summers. Chaparral ecosystems are found in many countries in the world. The only chaparrals in America are in California.

This ecosystem has a lot of fires. There are many plant and tree populations in the chaparral. Some are not hurt by fire. In fact, some plants need fire. Their seeds will only open and grow after a fire.

Animals in the chaparral can live where it is very dry. But they need the chaparral plants for water, food, and shelter.

The scrub jay and the horned lizard live in the chaparral.

Taiga

The **taiga** (TY guh) is another kind of ecosystem. It is found in the north. Taigas are very cold with long winters. Summers are short and cool. Taiga ecosystems are dry. Most of the water in a taiga comes from snow.

The trees in the taiga are evergreens. Evergreen trees stay green all year. Evergreen leaves help keep in water. Their needles do well in cold weather. Animals of the taiga also must like the cold. Moose and deer live in the taiga.

This taiga ecosystem is in Alaska.

MAIN IDEA AND DETAILS

Why do rainforests have so many types of plants and animals?

Summary Different land ecosystems have different nonliving parts. Use the chart to list two nonliving parts of each ecosystem discussed in this lesson.

Tropical Rainforest
a.
b.

Desert
a.
b.

Main Idea
Ecosystems differ because of the nonliving parts found in each type.

Taiga
a.
b.

Chaparral
a.
b.

Main Idea and Details Why do rainforests have so many types of plants and animals?

_____

_____

_____

_____

VOCABULARY

coral reef An ecosystem found in warm, tropical salt water and built on a structure of coral deposits. *(noun)*

VOCABULARY SKILL: Word Comparisons

Study the words *freshwater* and *saltwater*. What word part do they have in common?

_____

How does adding the word parts *fresh* and *salt* help these terms give more information about a water ecosystem?

_____

_____

4 What Are Some Water Ecosystems?

Organisms live in a water ecosystem because of its nonliving parts.

Saltwater Ecosystems

Ocean ecosystems have different nonliving parts. The shore is the place where the water meets the land. The shore might be covered by salt water. It might also get air and sunlight.

The plants and animals that live by the shore have to deal with both air and water. Clams are one of these animals. They stick to rocks so that waves cannot pull them out to sea.

Ocean Ecosystem

3.a. Students know ecosystems can be described by their living and nonliving parts.

After you pass the shore, you reach the coastal ocean. Plants here are very different than on shore. California's coastal ocean has giant underwater forests of kelp. Kelp is a tall, brown plant. Otters are one of the animals that live there.

A **coral** (KOR uhl) **reef** is another kind of underwater ecosystem. Coral are small animals that live in warm, sunny ocean water. They build hard shells. These shells connect with other coral shells and become the coral reef. Coral reefs are home to a lot of different plants and animals.

Shore

Sea stars and anemones live near the shore.

Coastal Ocean

In some parts of the coastal ocean, fish live in coral reefs.

1. List three nonliving parts found along the shore of an ocean ecosystem.

    a. _____

    b. _____

    c. _____

2. Both of these habitats are found in coastal oceans. List two characteristics of each habitat.

    Kelp Forest

    a. _____
    _____

    b. _____
    _____

    Coral Reef

    a. _____
    _____

    b. _____
    _____

3. List two reasons why algae are important to the open ocean ecosystem.

a. _____

b. _____

4. Organisms live at different levels in the open ocean. Next to each open ocean level, write the name or description of an organism that lives there.

a. Surface Level:

_____

b. Middle Level:

_____

c. Deep Level:

_____

Farther out past the coastal ocean is the open ocean. Simple, small plants called algae live in the open ocean. They are a very important part of the ocean. There are so many algae that they make most of Earth's oxygen. They also are food for other ocean animals.

Sunlight does not go deep into ocean water. Most of the ocean is dark and cold. Some organisms still live there. There are fish that can make their own light. They use the light to find food.

Open Ocean

Dolphins and whales spend most of their time near the surface.

Fangtooth fish live in the cold, dark, deep parts of the ocean.

Huge groups of fish live in the middle levels of the open ocean.

This bird lives in a freshwater ecosystem.

Freshwater Ecosystems

Other bodies of water are made of fresh water. Rivers, streams, lakes, and ponds all have fresh water.

Rivers and streams have water that flows, or moves. At the start of a river, the water moves fast. It looks clear. Fish that can swim fast live here. Farther along the river, the flow slows. Plants live here. Beavers and birds live here, too.

As the river flows, it picks up mud. At the end of the river, the water drops the mud and the river looks dirty. Catfish and other animals live in these dark waters.

5. List four bodies of water that are made up of fresh water.

a. _____

b. _____

c. _____

d. _____

6. Why does the water at the end of a river look dirty?

_____

_____

_____

_____

Summary   Different water ecosystems have their own sets of animals, plants, and nonliving parts. Use the Venn diagram to classify water ecosystems as saltwater or freshwater.

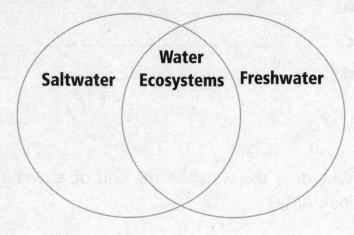

Saltwater   **Water Ecosystems**   Freshwater

Compare and Contrast   Compare three kinds of freshwater ecosystems.

_____

_____

_____

Ponds and lakes have still water. Still water does not move. Algae, insects, and fish live near the warm surface. Deeper down it is cool, but there is light. Small organisms in the water called plankton live here. Fish like to eat plankton.

In the deepest water of lakes, it is dark and cold. Organisms live here, too. They eat dead plants and animals that sink.

Fresh water lakes are home to many organisms.

COMPARE AND CONTRAST

Compare three kinds of freshwater ecosystems.

24

Glossary

chaparral (shap ur AL) An ecosystem with wet and mild winters and extremely hot and dry summer.

chaparral Ecosistema con inviernos templados y húmedos y veranos muy cálidos y secos.

community (kuh MYOO nih tee) All the organisms in an ecosystem.

comunidad Todos los organismos que componen un ecosistema.

coral reef (KOR uhl reef) An ecosystem found in warm, tropical salt water and built on a structure of coral deposits.

arrecife de coral Ecosistema que se encuentra en las aguas marinas tropicales y sobre una estructura de depósitos de coral.

desert (DEH zurt) A dry ecosystem with sandy soil.

desierto Ecosistema cálido y seco con suelo arenoso.

ecosystem (EE koh sihs tuhm) All the living and nonliving things that interact in an area.

ecosistema Todos los seres vivos y las cosas sin vida que interactúan en una misma zona.

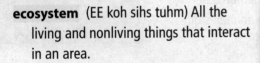

Group two or more of the words on the page and explain why they go together.

Write a single sentence using as many words from the page as you can.

Glossary

energy (EHN ur jee) The ability to cause change.

energía Capacidad de causar cambios.

environment (ehn VY ruhn muhnt) Everything that surrounds and affects an organism.

medio ambiente Todo lo que rodea y afecta a un organismo.

organism (AWR guh nihz uhm) A living thing.

organismo Ser vivo.

oxygen (AHK sih juhn) A gas most animals need to survive.

oxígeno El gas que necesitan la mayoría de los animales para sobrevivir.

population (pahp yuh LAY shun) All the members of one kind of plant or animal in a community.

población Todos los miembros del mismo tipo de plantas o animales que viven en una comunidad.

Glossary

rainforest (RAYN fawr ihst) An ecosystem where it rains a lot.

   bosque tropical Ecosistema donde llueve mucho.

reproduce (ree pruh DOOS) To make more organisms of their own kind.

   reproducir Cuando un ser vivo crea más organismos del mismo tipo.

taiga (TY guh) A fairly dry ecosystem with very cold, long winters and short, cool summers.

   taiga Ecosistema seco con inviernos muy largos y fríos y veranos cortos y frescos.

temperate zone (TEHM pur iht zohn) An area of Earth where the temperature rarely gets very hot or very cold.

   zona templada Zona de la Tierra donde la temperatura rara vez es muy cálida o muy fría.

 Visit www.eduplace.com to play puzzles and word games.

Circle the words in this Glossary that are the same in English and Spanish.

WHAT DID YOU LEARN?

Vocabulary

❶ ⟨Circle⟩ the correct answer on the page.

Comprehension

❷ _____
_____
_____

❸ _____
_____

❹ _____
_____
_____

Critical Thinking

❺ _____
_____
_____

Think About What You Have Read

Vocabulary

❶ All of the organisms of an ecosystem make up a/an _____.

A) community

B) environment

C) population

D) taiga

Comprehension

❷ An ecosystem is made up of _____.

❸ Nonliving conditions in a desert are _____.

❹ How do living things in an ecosystem interact?

Critical Thinking

❺ Explain the difference between an ecosystem and a community.

Interactions of Living Things

WHAT DO YOU KNOW?

Write or draw something about each of these topics.

a. How organisms depend on one another

_____

_____

b. How organisms are adapted to survive

_____

_____

c. How organisms compete _____

_____

_____

Contents

1 How Do Organisms Depend on
Each Other? 32

2 How Are Organisms Adapted
to Survive? 39

3 How Do Organisms Compete? 47

Glossary 52

WHAT DO YOU WANT TO KNOW?

Skim the pictures and headings in this chapter.
List one thing you want to find out about each
of these topics.

a. How organisms depend on each other:

_____

_____

b. How organisms are adapted to survive:

_____

_____

c. How organisms compete:

_____

_____

VOCABULARY

consumer An animal that gets energy by eating plants, or by eating other animals that eat plants. *(noun)*

pollinator An animal that helps plants make seeds by moving pollen. *(noun)*

producer An organism that makes its own food. *(noun)*

seed dispersal The scattering or carrying away of seeds from the plant that produced them. *(noun phrase)*

VOCABULARY SKILL: Sentence Context

You can use the other words in a sentence to figure out the meaning of a word. What is the meaning of the word *protected* in the sentence below? Underline other words that help you.

Their nests can stay hidden in the leaves, protected from hungry animals and the Sun.

2.a. Students know plants are the start of most food chains.
2.b. Students know producers and consumers (herbivores, carnivores, omnivores, and decomposers) are parts of food chains and food webs; they know these organisms may compete in an ecosystem.
3.c. Students know many plants depend on animals to pollinate them and spread their seed; animals depend on plants for food and shelter.

1 How Do Organisms Depend on Each Other?

Living things in an ecosystem depend on each other to get their needs met.

Interdependence

Living things in an ecosystem are interdependent (ihn tur dih PEHN duhnt). That means that they need each other to meet their needs. Some animals need plants for food. Organisms need each other for other things, too.

This bird needs plants for food.

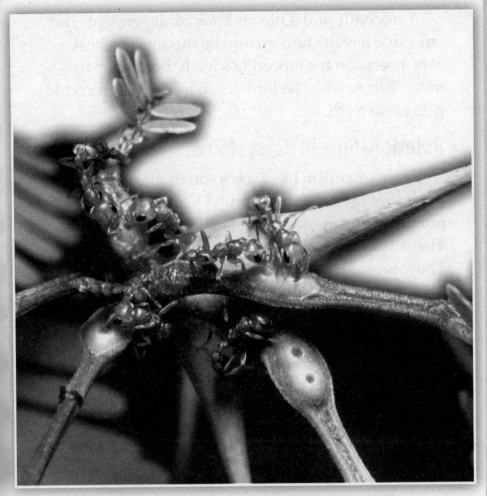

These stinging ants use the acacia tree as a home.

Plants are shelter for some animals. Animals protect some plants. The acacia tree and the stinging ant are interdependent. These ants live inside the tree. They eat a sugar made by the tree.

The tree also uses the ants. If another animal tries to eat the tree, the ants will bite it and chase it away.

1. Define the word *interdependent*.

_____

_____

2. The ants and the acacia tree are interdependent.

   a. How do the ants depend on the acacia tree?

   _____

   _____

   _____

   b. How does the acacia tree depend on the ants?

   _____

   _____

   _____

3. Compare and contrast a producer and a consumer.

Organisms in Ecosystems

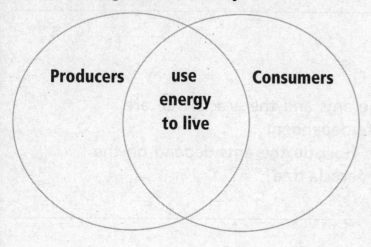

Producers | use energy to live | Consumers

I Wonder . . . Could animals survive on Earth without plants?

_____

_____

_____

A crocodile and a plover are interdependent. The crocodile lets the bird go into its mouth. The bird eats insects on the crocodile's teeth. Both animals meet their needs. The bird gets a meal. The crocodile gets clean teeth.

Relationships in Ecosystems

Every organism has a job to do in the ecosystem. Plants are the producers (pruh DOO surz). A **producer** is an organism that makes its own food. Plants use the energy from sunlight to make food. They use some of the energy from the food to grow. They use some energy to reproduce.

Some animals eat plants. They are consumers (kuhn SOO murz). A **consumer** gets energy by eating plants or by eating other animals. Consumers use this energy to live.

All consumers in an ecosystem need producers for food. Without producers, all other organisms would die.

These animals are interdependent.

California Redwood Forest

Plants are producers.

Animals are consumers.

4. Point to a consumer in the photo. How many can you find? List the names of the consumers below.

a. _____

b. _____

5. Which producers can you find in the photo? Write the names of three producers below.

a. _____

b. _____

c. _____

35

6. Shelter is a safe place for an organism to live.

a. How do trees provide shelter for animals?

_____

_____

_____

b. How do trees provide shelter for other plants?

_____

_____

_____

Trees provide shelter for many organisms.

Shelter is a basic need of all living things. Some animals get help from other organisms for their shelter. Many birds make their homes in tree branches. Their nests can stay hidden in the leaves, protected from hungry animals and the Sun.

Trees give shelter to other plants, too. Plants that grow best where it is wet and shady can find shelter near the trunk of a tree.

Pollinators and Seed Dispersal

In an ecosystem, some living things help others with reproduction (ree pruh DUHK shuhn). Reproduction is the life process of making offspring, or young. It is a basic need of all organisms.

Many plants reproduce by making seeds. To make seeds, a plant must move pollen (PAHL un) from one part of the flower to another. But how can a plant do this? Wind can carry pollen, but so can animals like insects and birds. An animal that helps plants make seeds by moving pollen is called a **pollinator** (PAHL uh nay tur). The animal moves the pollen while it eats.

Butterflies help to pollinate flowers.

7. Fill in the chart to explain how living things help each other with reproduction.

> **Reproduction**

a. Many plants reproduce by making _____ .

b. Plants make seeds when _____ is moved from one flower part to another.

c. _____ and _____ carry pollen.

d. An animal that helps plants make seeds by moving pollen is called a _____ .

8. When seeds are taken away from the plant that made them, _____ occurs.

9. List two ways in which seeds are dispersed.

a. _____

b. _____

Summary Living things in an ecosystem depend on one another for basic needs. List two basic needs below.

a. _____

b. _____

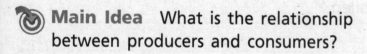

Main Idea What is the relationship between producers and consumers?

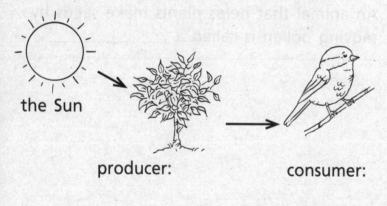

the Sun

producer: consumer:

_____   _____

_____   _____

_____   _____

_____   _____

Some plants need animals to carry their seeds to new places where they can grow. Taking the seeds away from the plant that made them is called **seed dispersal** (dih SPUR suhl).

Some seeds are carried by the wind. Some are carried by animals by mistake. This happens when an animal gets the seeds caught in its hair or fur. Some seeds grow inside of fruit. When animals eat the fruit, they will either drop the seed or the seed will come out as waste. Either way, the seed is dispersed.

This bird helps the plant to reproduce.

MAIN IDEA

What is the relationship between producers and consumers?

How Are Organisms Adapted to Survive?

2

Plants and animals must be adapted to their environment in order to survive.

Plant and Animal Adaptations

Some animals live in the water. Others live in the desert. Different plants and animals live in different environments. The place where a plant or animal lives is called its **habitat** (HAB ih tat). A shark's habitat is the ocean. A bird's habitat is the forest.

Plants and animals have **adaptations** (ad ap TAY-shuhnz). An adaptation is something a plant or animal has or does that helps it to live.

An adaptation is in all members of an organism. So if one wood duck has an adaptation, like sharp claws, then every wood duck has the adaptation. The wood duck is an example of a species (SPEE sheez). A **species** is a group of organisms that make the same kind of organisms.

VOCABULARY

adaptation A physical feature or behavior that helps a plant or animal survive. *(noun)*

camouflage The coloring, marking, or other physical appearance of an animal that helps it blend in with its surroundings. *(noun)*

extinction When all the members of a species die out. *(noun)*

habitat The place where a plant or animal lives. *(noun)*

hibernate Go into a deep sleep during which very little energy is used. *(verb)*

mimicry An adaptation that allows an animal to protect itself by looking like another kind of animal or like a plant. *(noun)*

predator Animals that hunt other animals for food. *(noun)*

prey Any animal that is hunted for food by a predator. *(noun)*

species A group of organisms that produces organisms of the same kind. *(noun)*

 3.b. Students know that in an environment, some kinds of plants and animals live well, some live less well, and some cannot live at all.

39

1. Find the pointed end of the leaf in the photo. How does the pointed end of a leaf help a plant survive in a rainforest habitat?

_____

_____

_____

2. Use your finger to trace the shape of the rabbit's ears in the photo. How do the rabbit's big ears help the animal to stay cool in the hot desert?

_____

_____

Adaptations to Habitat

FOREST The aye aye has big eyes that help it see in the dark. One of its fingers is very thin. It uses this finger to dig out food.

RAINFOREST Since water that stays on leaves can make plants sick, leaves have pointed ends that make the water drip off.

DESERT The rabbit's fur helps it to blend in. Its big ears release heat and keep the rabbit cool.

TUNDRA The ox's thick fur helps it stay warm.

Some animals hunt and eat other animals for food. These animals are called **predators** (PREH deh-turz). **Prey** (PRAY) are the animals that are hunted for food by a predator.

The bear is a predator. The fish is its prey.

3. Study the photo of the bear. Now fill in the blanks.

a. Because it hunts and eats the fish, the bear is a _____.

b. Bears hunt fish for food. Fish are the _____ of bear.

I Wonder . . . Can an animal be both predator and prey? What do you think? Give an example to support your idea.

_____

_____

_____

_____

4. Some adaptations are physical. They affect how an animal looks.

a. What adaptation is camouflage?

_____

_____

b. How do predators and prey use camouflage?

_____

_____

5. In the photo of the butterfly, find the two large spots on the butterfly's wings.

a. Write the definition of *mimicry*.

_____

_____

_____

b. What do the butterfly's two large spots look like?

_____

_____

Physical Adaptations

Some animals look like their environment. They are hard to see. This adaptation is called camouflage (KAM uh flahzh). **Camouflage** is the color, spots, or marks on an animal that help it blend in with its environment. Animals use camouflage to hide from predators or from prey.

Some insects protect themselves by using mimicry (MIHM ih kree). **Mimicry** is an adaptation that protects the animal by making it look like another plant or animal. The owl butterfly has large spots on its wings that look like the eyes of an owl. These spots scare away birds that would eat the butterfly.

The owl butterfly uses mimicry to scare away predators.

A deer's light brown fur and white spots look like sunlight and shade.

This fish catches insects by shooting them with water.

Behavior

A behavior can help a predator as it hunts. Some animals hunt in groups. This behavior helps trap a prey so it cannot easily escape.

Behavior can also help prey. Rabbits run zigzag. This helps them dodge predators and escape.

Different ecosystems get very cold in the winter. Some animals have an adaptation that helps them live through this cold. They **hibernate** (HY bur nayt), or go into a deep sleep. As they hibernate they use very little energy and do not need to eat.

6. Use your finger to trace the stream of water from the fish's mouth to the insect. How does this behavior help a fish survive?

_____

_____

I Wonder . . . How does flying help a bird survive in its habitat? What do you think?

_____

_____

_____

_____

7. What are two things that can happen to an organism when its habitat changes?

a. _____

b. _____

8. Falcons usually build their nests high in trees. In some cities, trees have been cut down to build high buildings. How have falcons adapted to this change?

_____

_____

Surviving Change

Organisms count on their habitat to give them all the things they need to live. So what happens when a habitat changes?

If a habitat changes, then a plant or animal might die. But some organisms survive when their habitats change. These species have adaptations that help them live after the changes.

A falcon is a large bird. It makes its nest high up in trees. Now, these birds build nests on high buildings in American cities. This is how they adapt to change.

A falcon sits on a building in Los Angeles.

Many species cannot meet their needs when their habitat changes. They do not have adaptations that let them.

Pandas eat bamboo. Bamboo is a long, hard plant. Pandas cannot live without bamboo. This is very dangerous for the panda. Bamboo forests in the panda's habitat are being cut down. Without bamboo forests, wild pandas will not live.

Pandas need bamboo to survive.

15

9. Complete the sequence diagram.

Pandas eat _____.

Bamboo forests are being _____.

Without bamboo, pandas _____.

10. How can people prevent pandas from dying?

_____

_____

45

11. Look at the photo of the passenger pigeon. These birds are extinct.

a. What does *extinction* mean?

_____

b. What caused passenger pigeons to become extinct?

_____

_____

_____

Summary Plants and animals have adaptations that help them meet their needs. Adaptations can be physical features or behaviors.

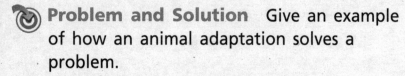 **Problem and Solution** Give an example of how an animal adaptation solves a problem.

Problem	Solution

Extinction

What if the panda's habitat were gone? Pandas would probably become extinct (ihk STIHNKT). **Extinction** is when all the members of a species die. Any species can become extinct if they cannot adapt to change.

Passenger pigeons are a type of bird. They used to have a large population. Over time, the forests they lived in were cut down. This changed their habitat. Then they became a prey of humans. Now they are extinct.

Habitat change is still a big danger to animals all over the world.

passenger pigeon

PROBLEM AND SOLUTION

Give an example of how an animal adaptation solves a problem.

How Do Organisms Compete?

Food, air, water, and living space are resources. In an ecosystem animals compete for resources.

Competing for Food and Water

Organisms need food and water. They need air and living space. Organisms compete for resources (REE sor sehz). A **resource** is something useful. There are not enough resources.

In a pond, frogs are food for several different kinds of animals. If there are not enough frogs, animals that eat them may die.

Snakes, birds, and raccoons compete with each other to eat frogs.

snake

raccoon

shore bird

frog

VOCABULARY

resource Something found in nature that is useful to organisms. *(noun)*

VOCABULARY SKILL: Prefix/Suffix

The prefix *re-* means "again." Read the definition of *resource* above. How is the meaning of the prefix *re-* contained in the word *resource*?

_____

_____

1. Look at the picture of the pond and the animals.
   a. What kinds of animals eat frogs?

   _____

   b. What might happen if there are not enough frogs in the pond?

   _____

 2.b. Students know producers and consumers (herbivores, carnivores, omnivores, and decomposers) are parts of food chains and food webs; they know these organisms may compete in an ecosystem.

2. The birds in the photo are competing for living space on the cliffs. The cliffs are very crowded.

a. If the cliffs are too crowded, what might happen to some of the birds?

_____

_____

b. How will this change affect the population size of the birds?

_____

_____

The Murre birds' living space is very crowded.

Competing for Living Space

Living space is an important resource. Organisms compete for it. If a place is too crowded, some will die. This competition keeps the size of the population low.

Some birds raise their young in places that are safe from predators. They use places like cliffs or beaches. But these places might get too crowded. Birds may not be able to find a spot for a nest. If they have to leave, the place they go might not be safe. They and their young will be in danger from predators.

Forests are full of trees and plants that compete for food and sunlight. Some plants have adaptations that let them reach for the light. Others have long roots that can reach for the soil. Others have no roots. They get nutrients from the air and water around them.

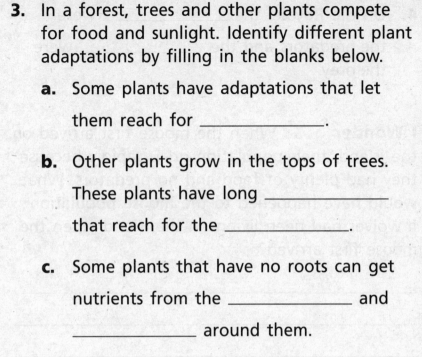

3. In a forest, trees and other plants compete for food and sunlight. Identify different plant adaptations by filling in the blanks below.

a. Some plants have adaptations that let them reach for _____.

b. Other plants grow in the tops of trees. These plants have long _____ that reach for the _____.

c. Some plants that have no roots can get nutrients from the _____ and _____ around them.

4. On Isle Royale, the _____ were the predators and the _____ were the prey.

I Wonder . . . When the moose first arrived on the island, their population grew rapidly because they had plenty of food and no predators. What would have happened to the moose population if wolves had been living on the island when the moose first arrived?

_____

_____

_____

_____

A Balanced Ecosystem

In an ecosystem, populations are always changing. Old animals die. New animals are born. When a tree falls, others grow to take its place. When an ecosystem is balanced, there are enough resources for all the living things.

In a balanced ecosystem, the numbers of predators and prey stay about the same. But sometimes this balance is upset. That can lead to major problems for the populations.

An example of a predator and prey problem happened on an island named Isle Royale. Moose lived on the island for a long time. After they had lived on the island for thirty years with no predators, their population was huge. Then it dropped quickly. Many moose began to die. They died so fast because there was not enough food for all of them.

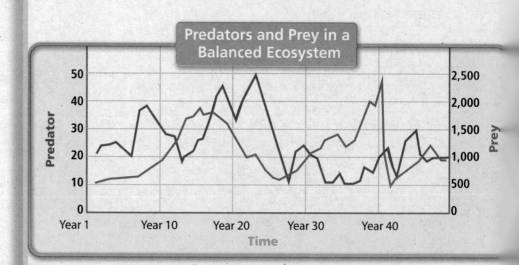

Predators and Prey in a Balanced Ecosystem

Populations of predators and prey tend to rise and fall together.

Wolves are predators of the moose. They came to the island to hunt and eat the moose. Very quickly, the number of moose dropped and the number of wolves grew. But then the wolves' numbers began to drop. They had eaten too many moose. Now, there weren't enough moose left for all of them to eat. When the wolves began to die, more moose were able to live. There were less wolves to hunt them. The populations of these species rise and fall as they try to find a balance.

CAUSE AND EFFECT

How would a decrease in predators affect the prey?

Summary   The populations of predators and prey are in balance in a healthy ecosystem. Complete the diagram below to show how ecosystems remain in balance.

When the wolf population decreases,

the moose population _____.

the moose population _____.

When the wolf population _____,

Cause and Effect   How would a decrease in predators affect the prey?

_____

_____

_____

51

Choose a glossary term and draw a picture to illustrate it.

adaptation (ad ap TAY shun) A physical feature or a behavior that helps a plant or animal survive.

adaptación Rasgo físico o comportamiento que ayuda a sobrevivir a una planta o a un animal.

camouflage (KAM uh flahzh) The coloring, marking, or other physical appearance of an animal that helps it blend in with its surroundings.

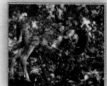

camuflaje La coloración, marcas u otra apariencia física de un animal, que le ayudan a esconderse en sus alrededores.

consumer (kuhn SOO muhr) An animal that gets energy by eating plants, or by eating other animals that eat plants.

consumidor Animal que obtiene energía alimentándose de plantas, o alimentándose de otros animales que comen plantas.

extinction (ihk STIHNK shun) When all the members of a species die out.

extinción Cuando mueren todos los miembros de una especie.

habitat (HAB ih tat) The place where a plant or animal lives.

hábitat Lugar donde viven las plantas o los animales.

Glossary

hibernate (HY bur nayt) Go into a deep sleep during which very little energy is used.

hibernar Entrar en un sueño profundo, durante el cual se gasta muy poca energía.

mimicry (MIHM ih kree) An adaptation that allows an animal to protect itself by looking like another kind of animal or like a plant.

mimetismo Adaptación que protege a un animal por el parecido de éste con otra planta o animal.

pollinator (PAHL uh nay tur) An animal that helps plants make seeds by moving pollen.

polinizador Animal que transporta el polen de un sitio a otro ayudando a las plantas a fabricar semillas.

predator (PREH deh tur) Animals that hunt other animals for food.

depredador Animales que cazan a otros animales para alimentarse.

prey (PRAY) Any animal that is hunted for food by a predator.

presa Cualquier animal que un depredador caza para alimentarse.

prey   predator

Group two or more of the words on the page and explain why they go together.

Visit www.eduplace.com to play puzzles and word games.

Find the English words that are like these Spanish words. List these words in the chart.

English	Spanish
	adaptación
	hábitat
	productor

Glossary

producer (pruh DOO sur) An organism that makes its own food.

productor Organismo que produce su propio alimento.

resource (REE sors) Something found in nature that is useful to organisms.

recurso Algo que se encuentra en la naturaleza y que es útil para los organismos.

seed dispersal (SEED dih SPUR suhl) The scattering or carrying away of seeds from the plant that produced them.

dispersión de semillas Esparcimiento de las semillas lejos de la planta que las produjo.

species (SPEE sheez) A group of organisms that produces organisms of the same kind.

especie Grupo de organismos que producen organismos del mismo tipo.

Think About What You Have Read

Vocabulary

❶ The scattering of seeds is called _____.

A) adaptation

B) mimicry

C) pollinator

D) seed dispersal

Comprehension

❷ When certain animals go into a deep sleep over the winter, they _____.

❸ Why do plants and animals compete for resources?

❹ What would happen if all the frogs in a pond died?

Critical Thinking

❺ How can an animal be both predator and prey?

WHAT DID YOU LEARN?

Vocabulary

❶ Circle the correct answer on the page.

Comprehension

❷ _____

❸ _____

_____

❹ _____

_____

Critical Thinking

❺ _____

_____

_____

_____

KWL

WHAT DO YOU KNOW?

List one fact about each topic:

a. Food chains _____

_____

b. Food webs _____

_____

c. Microorganisms _____

_____

Energy in Ecosystems

Contents

1 What Are Food Chains? 58

2 What Are Food Webs? 64

3 What Are Microorganisms? 67

Glossary 71

WHAT DO YOU WANT TO KNOW?

Skim the pictures and headings in this chapter. List one thing you want to find out about each of these topics:

a. Food chains _____

_____

b. Food webs _____

_____

c. Microorganisms _____

_____

VOCABULARY

carnivore An animal that eats only other animals. *(noun)*

food chain The path of food energy in an ecosystem from plants to animals. *(noun)*

herbivore An animal that eats only plants. *(noun)*

omnivore An animal that eats both plants and animals. *(noun)*

photosynthesis The process through which plants make their own food. *(noun)*

VOCABULARY SKILL: Root Words

The Greek root *photo* means "light," and the Greek root *syntithenai* means "to put together." Combine the meanings of these root words to write your own definition of *photosynthesis*.

_____

_____

2.a. Students know plants are the start of most food chains.
2.b. Students know producers and consumers (herbivores, carnivores, omnivores, and decomposers) are parts of food chains and food webs; they know these organisms may compete in an ecosystem.

1 What Are Food Chains?

In an ecosystem, energy goes from the Sun to producers. Then energy goes from producers to consumers.

Energy from the Sun

All living things need energy. They get that energy from food. Some animals eat plants. Some animals eat other animals.

Plants do not eat food. They make their own food. They do this by **photosynthesis** (foh toh SIHN-thih sihs). Photosynthesis takes place in a plant's leaves. The leaves trap energy from the Sun. During photosynthesis, plants use water and a gas from the air to make sugar. Sugar is their food.

Sun

Plants get energy from the Sun.

Plant

Predator and Prey

As you have learned, an animal that eats other animals for food is a predator. A fox is a predator. A rabbit is its prey. An animal can be both predator and prey. A fox eats rabbits, but other animals eat foxes.

Plants are producers. Animals are consumers. When a consumer, such as a rabbit, eats a plant, it gets some of the plant's energy. When the rabbit is eaten by the fox, the fox gets some of the plant's energy.

Predator

Prey

1. Find the fox in the picture. How can the fox be both predator and prey?

_____

_____

_____

I Wonder . . . Plants are producers that get energy from the Sun. A fox is a consumer. As a consumer, how does a fox receive some of the Sun's energy in the food it eats?

_____

_____

_____

_____

59

2. Trace the path of energy in an ecosystem by completing the diagram below.

In every ecosystem . . .

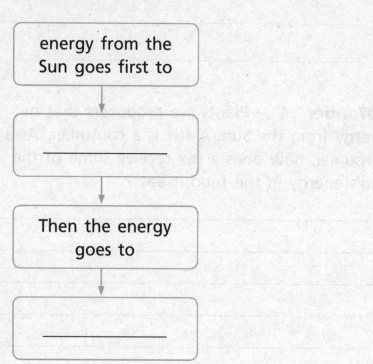

energy from the
Sun goes first to

_____

↓

Then the energy
goes to

_____

In a pond, tiny plants are the producers. They use energy from the Sun to make food. Small animals then eat the small plants. These small animals are in turn eaten by small fish. Then the small fish get eaten by big fish.

In every ecosystem, energy comes from the Sun. First it goes to the producers. Then it goes to the consumers. The energy goes from one stage to the next.

This bird catches its prey.

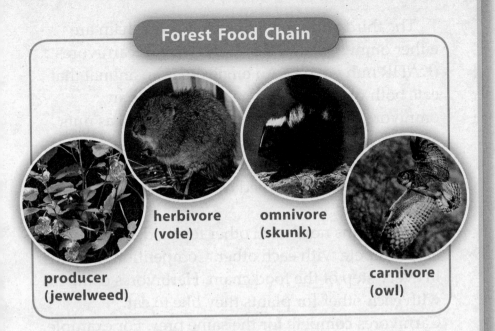

Forest Food Chain

producer
(jewelweed)

herbivore
(vole)

omnivore
(skunk)

carnivore
(owl)

Food Chains

A **food chain** (CHAYN) shows how food energy goes from plants to animals. In the food chain above, a vole gets energy by eating a plant. Then the skunk gets energy by eating the vole. And an owl gets energy from eating the skunk.

Food chains are different in different ecosystems. But the first part is always a producer. Most producers are green plants. Energy enters the food chain through the plant. This happens when the plant uses the sunlight for photosynthesis. Plants make food by photosynthesis.

Then the plants are eaten by animals. Animals that eat only plants are called **herbivores** (HUR buh vawrz). Herbivores get energy from eating the plants.

3. What is the first part of every food chain?

_____

What kind of living things are most producers?

_____

4. Draw a star over the photo of the herbivore in the forest food chain.

a. Write the definition of an herbivore.

_____

b. Where would you find an herbivore in a food chain?

_____

_____

5. Some animals eat both plants and animals.

   a. An animal that eats both plants and animals is called an _____.

   b. Which animal shown eats both plants and animals? _____

6. If an animal eats only other animals, it is called a _____.

7. Label each level of the energy pyramid. Use the terms *producers*, *herbivores*, and *carnivores*.

I Wonder . . . As a living organism, you must eat food in order to survive. Are you an herbivore, an omnivore, or a carnivore? What do you think?

_____

_____

_____

62

The third and fourth links in a food chain are either omnivores (AHM nuh vawrz) or carnivores (KAHR nuh vawrz). An **omnivore** is an animal that eats both plants and animals. A skunk is an omnivore. It eats insects and mice, as well as nuts and berries.

A **carnivore** is an animal that eats only other animals. The great horned owl is a carnivore. It will not eat plants.

Organisms need each other for food. But they also compete with each other. Competition happens in every step of the food chain. Herbivores compete with each other for plants they like to eat. Carnivores compete for the same prey. For example, seagulls eat fish and crabs. But seals also eat fish and crabs. So seagulls and seals compete for fish and crabs in the ocean.

An omnivore eats both plants and animals.

A carnivore eats only other animals.

The Energy Pyramid

At each link in the food chain, some energy is lost. Plants use some energy to make flowers and seeds. So not all of the energy captured from the Sun goes to an animal that eats a plant. The animal that eats the plant uses some energy to look for food and run from predators. When that animal is eaten, even less of the energy is there for the predator that catches it.

In a food chain, the further an organism is from the producer, or plant, the less energy it gets when it eats. That is why the population of predators is smaller than the population of their prey. That is also why there are only three or four links on a food chain.

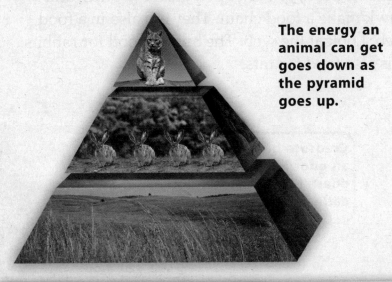

The energy an animal can get goes down as the pyramid goes up.

Summary In an ecosystem, energy flows from the Sun to producers and from producers to consumers.

Complete the diagram to tell how plants and some animals get energy.

A plant's leaves trap the Sun's _____.

↓

Plants make food through _____.

↓

Plants use water and a gas from the air to make _____ during photosynthesis.

↓

To get energy, animals eat _____ or other _____ that eat plants.

↓

A _____ would be at the top of the energy pyramid.

Sequence How are a predator and its prey related?

_____

_____

food web The overlap of two or more food chains. *(noun)*

VOCABULARY SKILL: Multiple-Meaning Words

The word *web* has many meanings, such as a *spider web* and the *World Wide Web*, or *Internet*. Think about the definition of the word *food chain*. Now use that definition, and your knowledge of the multiple meanings of *web*, to write your own definition for *food web*.

_____

_____

_____

2 What Are Food Webs?

Ecosystems have many food chains. They have food webs, too. A food web is made up of several food chains.

Chains and Webs

Ecosystems have plants and animals. Each organism is part of more than one food chain. Two or more food chains that overlap make a **food web**. In a food web, organisms are part of more than one food chain.

Look at the bush below. It is a creosote bush. The creosote bush, grasshopper, flicker (a bird), and hawk make a food chain. They are also in a food web. Look at the web. The bush is food for rabbits. It is also food for rats.

> Creosote bushes give off an odor like tar, but that doesn't stop animals from eating them.

A Desert Food Web

The hawk can soar over the desert and spot prey from far away.

The flicker catches insects with its tongue.

The creosote grasshopper feeds only on this kind of bush.

This rat eats the seeds of the creosote bush.

This rabbit moves quickly to escape its predators.

1. Find the creosote bush in the photo. Use your finger to trace the different energy paths that begin with the creosote bush. How many energy paths did you trace?

   _____

   List the organisms that receive energy directly from the creosote bush.

   a. _____

   b. _____

   c. _____

2. In the diagram below, use your pencil to circle the organisms that are part of several overlapping food chains.

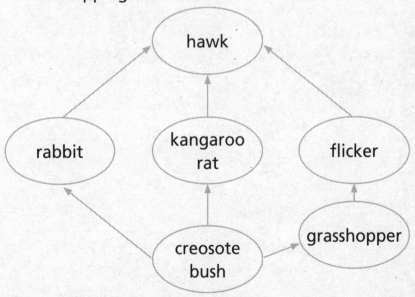

Summary A food web is made up of several food chains. In every kind of ecosystem, energy enters food webs through producers that are either green plants or plant-like organisms, such as algae.

Look at the ocean food web on this page. Plant-like organisms are producers. Which plant-like organisms are the producers in this food web?

_____

_____

 Sequence What is a food web?

_____

_____

An Ocean Food Web

Algae are producers.

Seagulls feed on fish and krill

Krill, small shrimp-like animals, are food for fish, birds, and mammals.

Small fish are food for birds, big fish, and some whales.

Some whales eat krill. Others eat fish.

Big fish eat smaller fish.

Sharks eat almost any fish.

SEQUENCE

What is a food web?

What Are Microorganisms?

3

Microorganisms are an important part of many ecosystems. Many help make food. Some are at the bottom of food chains.

One-Celled Organisms

A **cell** is the basic unit of life. Some small organisms only have one cell. Others have many cells. Organisms that are too small to be seen without a microscope are called **microorganisms** (my kroh AWR guh nihz uhmz). Organisms with one cell are microorganisms. Bacteria and yeast are microorganisms.

Bacteria (bak TEER ee uh) are microorganisms found all over Earth. There are good and bad bacteria. Some make you sick. Others are important for life.

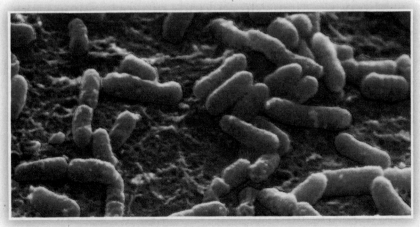

Some bacteria help your body get nutrients. Others make you sick.

VOCABULARY

bacteria Microorganisms found in all living organisms and everywhere on Earth. *(noun)*

cell The basic unit that makes up all living things. *(noun)*

microorganism An organism that cannot be seen without the help of a microscope. *(noun)*

plankton Microorganisms that exist in the water and form the beginning of most aquatic food chains. *(noun)*

VOCABULARY SKILL: Prefixes

The word *microorganism* contains the prefix *micro-*, which means "small." Use this definition and your knowledge of the word *organism* to write your own definition for *microorganism*.

_____

 2.a. Students know plants are the start of most food chains.
3.d. Students know that most microorganisms do not cause disease and that many are helpful.

67

1. Bacteria and yeast are microorganisms.
Bacteria help make these foods.

a. _____

b. _____

c. _____

Yeast is used to make this food rise.

_____

Yeast is used to make alcohol that helps make this fuel burn cleaner.

_____

2. Bacteria help you get _____ from the food you eat.

Bacteria turn dead _____ and _____ into _____ that are useful to living things.

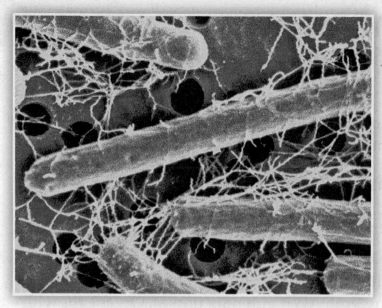

This microorganism helps turn milk into yogurt and cheese.

Microorganisms at Work

Microorganisms do all kinds of work. Some foods are made by bacteria. Bacteria help make yogurt, sour cream, and cheese.

Yeast is another microorganism. Yeast is used to make bread. Yeast eats the sugar in bread dough. This is what makes bread rise. Yeast also can be used to make alcohol that helps gasoline burn cleaner. This is good for the environment.

Without bacteria in your body, you would not be able to get all the nutrients in the food you eat. Bacteria also turn dead plants and animals into nutrients.

Microorganisms in Water

Most of Earth is covered by oceans. Plankton are found in the water of the oceans. **Plankton** are microorganisms that live in water. They make the beginning of most ocean food chains.

There are different kinds of plankton. Together, they form a layer over all of Earth's oceans.

Plankton produce the food that is the beginning of many ocean food chains.

3. You learned about food chains in Lesson 1. What role do plankton play in most ocean food chains?

_____

_____

I Wonder . . . Plankton produce the food with which many ocean food chains begin. What would happen to these food chains if all of Earth's plankton died?

_____

_____

_____

_____

Summary   Microorganisms are an important and necessary part of most ecosystems.

Microorganisms help you get nutrients from your food. Animals need oxygen to breathe. How do microorganisms help provide oxygen?

_____

_____

🎯 **Main Idea**   Why are microorganisms important in ocean food chains?

_____

_____

_____

Many kinds of plankton are small plants or one-celled algae (AL jee). Algae use the Sun's energy to make food. They do this by using photosynthesis. In photosynthesis, the plants give off oxygen. Because there are so many plankton in the world, they make most of the oxygen on Earth.

Ocean food webs need plankton. Without plankton using photosynthesis to make food, other animals could not live. Larger ocean animals, from fish to whales, eat plankton.

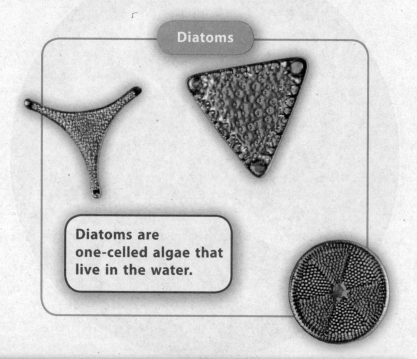

Diatoms

Diatoms are one-celled algae that live in the water.

MAIN IDEA

Why are microorganisms important in ocean food chains?

bacteria (bak TEER ee uh) Microorganisms found in all living organisms and everywhere on Earth.

bacteria Microorganismos que se hallan en todos los organismos vivos y en todos los lugares de la Tierra.

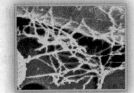

carnivore (KAHR nuh vawr) An animal that eats only other animals.

carnívoro Animal que sólo se alimenta de otros animales.

cell (sel) The basic unit that makes up all living things.
célula Unidad básica de la que se componen todos los seres vivos.

food chain (food chayn) The path of food energy in an ecosystem from plants to animals.

cadena alimenticia Recorrido que en un ecosistema sigue la energía de la comida, desde las plantas a los animales.

food web (food web) The overlap of two or more food chains.

red alimenticia Superposición de dos o más cadenas alimenticias.

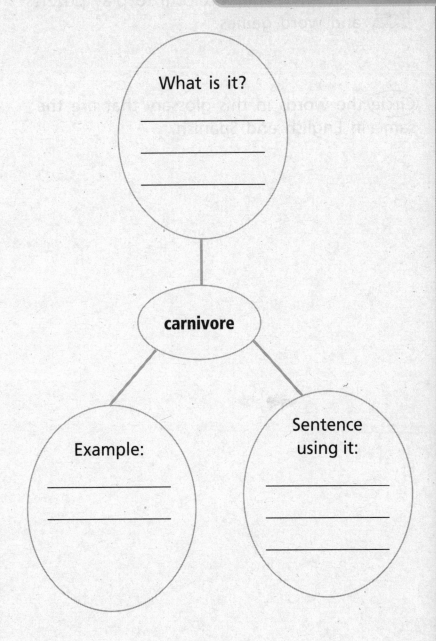

What is it?

_____

_____

_____

carnivore

Example:

_____

_____

Sentence using it:

_____

_____

_____

Visit www.eduplace.com to play puzzles and word games.

Circle the words in this glossary that are the same in English and Spanish.

Glossary

herbivore (HUR buh vawr) An animal that eats only plants.

herbívoro Animal que sólo come plantas.

microorganism (my kroh AWR guh nihz uhm) An organism that cannot be seen without the help of a microscope.

microorganismo Organismo que no se puede ver sin la ayuda de un microscopio.

omnivore (AHM nuh vawr) An animal that eats both plants and animals.

omnívoro Animal que se alimenta de otros animales y plantas.

photosynthesis (foh toh SIHN thih sihs) The process through which plants make their own food.

fotosíntesis Proceso por el cual las plantas fabrican su propio alimento.

plankton (PLANK tuhn) Microorganisms that exist in the water and form the beginning of most aquatic food chains.

plancton Microorganismos que existen en el agua y que forman el primer eslabón de la mayoría de las cadenas alimenticias acuáticas.

Responding

Think About What You Have Read

Vocabulary

❶ An animal that eats only plants is a/an _____.

  A) bacteria

  B) carnivore

  C) herbivore

  D) plankton

Comprehension

❷ Plants make food through the process of _____.

❸ An organism that can be seen only with a microscope is a/an _____.

❹ How are microorganisms helpful?

Critical Thinking

❺ How does an herbivore benefit from the Sun's energy?

WHAT DID YOU LEARN?

Vocabulary

❶ Circle the correct answer on the page.

Comprehension

❷ _____

❸ _____

❹ _____

_____

_____

Critical Thinking

❺ _____

_____

_____

Matter in Ecosystems

KWL

WHAT DO YOU KNOW?

List one fact about each of these topics:

a. How matter is cycled in an ecosystem

_____

_____

_____

b. How people affect ecosystems

_____

_____

_____

c. How ecosystems can be conserved

_____

_____

_____

Contents

1 How Is Matter Cycled in an Ecosystem? . . 76

2 How Do People Affect Ecosystems? 84

3 How Can Ecosystems Be Conserved? . . . 88

Glossary 96

WHAT DO YOU WANT TO KNOW?

Skim the pictures and the headings in this chapter. List one thing you want to find out about each of these topics.

a. The ways in which matter is cycled in an ecosystem

_____

_____

_____

b. The effects that people have on ecosystems

_____

_____

_____

VOCABULARY

compost Decayed material from once-living things that is used to enrich the soil. *(noun)*

decay To break down into simpler materials. *(verb)*

decomposer A living thing that breaks down the remains of dead organisms. *(noun)*

nutrient recycling The process of breaking down materials into a different form that can be used again. *(noun)*

scavenger An animal that feeds on the remains or wastes of dead animals. *(noun)*

VOCABULARY SKILL: Multiple-Meaning Words

Some words have more than one meaning. For example, the verb *release* can mean "to set free," or "published." Which meaning of *release* is intended in the following sentence?

Bacteria release nutrients into the soil.

2.b. Students know producers and consumers (herbivores, carnivores, omnivores, and decomposers) are parts of food chains and food webs; they know these organisms may compete in an ecosystem.
2.c. Students know decomposers recycle matter from dead plants and animals.
3.d. Students know that most microorganisms do not cause disease and that many are helpful.

1 How Is Matter Cycled in an Ecosystem?

Scavengers and decomposers are organisms that reuse dead plants and animals. They turn a dead organism into something that can be used by the rest of the ecosystem.

Scavengers

A **scavenger** (SKAV uhn jur) is an animal that eats the body or waste of dead animals. Predators look for living prey. Scavengers do not. Scavengers want animals that are dead.

Scavengers are consumers. They get energy from food. But a scavenger does not kill its food. It eats what is already dead. A scavenger will eat what is left of an animal that was killed by a predator. Raccoons and vultures are scavengers.

These beetles lay their eggs in dead animals. Their young use the dead body for food.

Scavengers in Food Webs

Predators are carnivores. They hunt and kill animals for food. Scavengers are also carnivores. They eat what is left by the predators. When a wolf kills a moose, it cannot eat all of the meat. What is left makes a meal for the scavengers.

This bird is both a carnivore and a scavenger.

1. You have learned about herbivores, carnivores, and omnivores in an earlier chapter. Explain which of these terms best describes a scavenger.

_____

_____

_____

I Wonder . . . Scavengers eat the remains of dead animals. What might happen if there were no scavengers? What do you think?

_____

_____

_____

2. What is the relationship between scavengers and nutrients in an ecosystem?

_____

_____

_____

3. Name an ocean scavenger.

_____

Most people think of this animal as a predator. When is it a scavenger?

_____

_____

_____

This animal, a peccarie, is like a pig. It is an omnivore. It will eat almost anything.

Without scavengers, many nutrients would be wasted. Scavengers help keep nutrients in the food chain. If a scavenger becomes prey, its nutrients are passed along. This is one reason that scavengers are important.

There are scavengers in every ecosystem. In the ocean, sharks are scavengers. Sharks are also predators. They hunt and kill animals. But sharks will also eat animals that are not alive. This makes them scavengers.

Decomposers

Decomposers (dee kuhm POH zurz) have an important job in the ecosystem. **Decomposers** break down what is left of dead organisms. Bacteria can be decomposers. Fungi (FUHN jy) is another group of organisms that are decomposers. Fungi include mold and mushrooms.

Some kinds of mold and bacteria cause disease. Mold can cause food to go bad. But most kinds of mold and bacteria are helpful, not harmful. A decomposer is helpful to the environment.

Many dead organisms are eaten by scavengers. Some are not. The ones that are not eaten **decay** (dih KAY), or break down into simpler materials. Decomposers help organisms to decay. All food chains end with decomposers.

This mushroom is a decomposer.

4. Finish the diagram to list organisms that are decomposers.

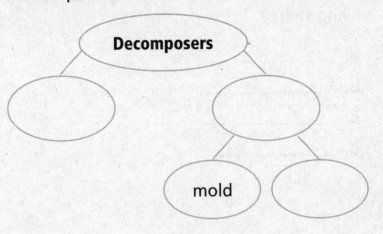

Decomposers

mold

5. What happens to dead organisms that are not eaten by scavengers?

_____

_____

6. You see a fallen log as you hike in the woods. What decomposers might you find living there?

a. _____

b. _____

c. _____

d. _____

7. Look at the picture of the rotting log. List three decomposers shown.

a. _____

b. _____

c. _____

A fallen tree is a good place to find decomposers. These decomposers break down wood. Insects such as ants and termites dig holes in the log. The holes make the log weak. Fungi and bacteria might be found on a log, too. Fungi break down dead plants and dead animals.

Decomposers help the log decay. This helps new plants grow. Nutrients from the dead wood are put back in the soil by decomposers. Decomposers break down materials so that nutrients can be reused. This is called **nutrient recycling**.

A Home for Many Living Things

This log provides food and shelter for the decomposers, scavengers, producers, herbivores, and carnivores living on it.

oyster fungus

beetle

ant

salamander

Nutrient recycling is very important for the ecosystem. Nutrients released by decomposers make the soil rich, which helps plants. Decomposers also help clean up the environment. They keep it from filling up with the bodies of dead plants and animals.

How fast something decays depends on its environment. Decay happens fastest in warm and wet places. Most decomposers need warmth and water to survive. In cold places, decay happens slowly. This is because few decomposers live in cold and dry environments.

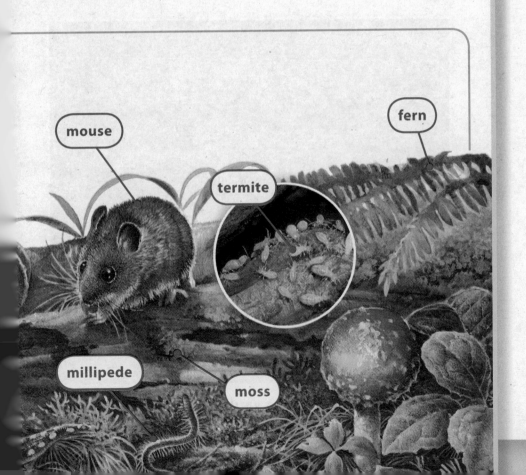

mouse

termite

fern

millipede

moss

8. List two reasons that decomposers are important to ecosystems.

a. _____

_____

_____

_____

_____

b. _____

_____

_____

_____

9. Circle the words that describe an environment in which decay happens fastest.

cold   wet   warm   dry

81

10. Decomposers help the environment in many ways.

   a. How can you help decomposers grow?

   _____

   _____

   _____

   b. What is compost?

   _____

   _____

11. Look at the circle graph. List three types of garbage you can put in a compost pile.

   a. _____

   b. _____

   c. _____

   What percentage of garbage can be composted?

   d. _____

Composting

Decomposers are important to ecosystems. They release nutrients that other organisms need to survive. They also make space. When plants and animals decay, the space they took up becomes free for other organisms.

Because decomposers are helpful, it makes sense to help them grow. People can make a perfect place for decomposers. They can do this by making a place where natural material, including garbage, can become compost (KAHM pohst). **Compost** is decayed material that is used to make the soil rich.

This compost pile includes yard waste and food scraps.

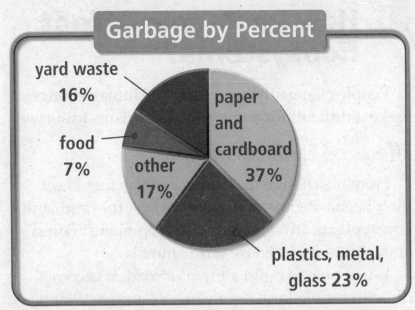

Garbage by Percent

yard waste 16%

food 7%

other 17%

paper and cardboard 37%

plastics, metal, glass 23%

Food, yard waste, paper, and cardboard can go into compost piles. As this chart shows, 60% of all garbage can be composted.

Materials that could be used in a compost pile are often thrown away. If these materials end up at a landfill, they take up space and decay very slowly.

Grass clippings, leaves, kitchen scraps, and some paper should be put into compost piles. These things are recycled by decomposers. After the decomposers have broken down the compost pile, the decayed leftovers can be mixed with the soil. This soil will be very rich and will help plants grow.

CAUSE AND EFFECT

What is one way that decomposers are helpful?

Summary Organisms such as scavengers and decomposers recycle matter from dead plants and animals. They turn this matter into a form that can be used by other organisms.

Complete the diagram to compare scavengers and predators.

Scavenger   **Predator**

- eats remains of

  _____

- may eat remains of animals killed by predator

- takes in

  _____

  that would be wasted

- consumers

- get energy from

  _____

- carnivores eat _____

- hunts and kills other animals for

  _____

- does not always eat all parts of prey

Cause and Effect What is one way that decomposers are helpful?

_____

_____

_____

83

VOCABULARY

hazardous waste Waste that can pollute the environment even when it occurs in very small amounts. *(noun)*

litter Trash that is not disposed of in a way that prevents harm to ecosystems. *(noun)*

pollutant A material that causes pollution. *(noun)*

pollution The addition of harmful materials to the environment. *(noun)*

VOCABULARY SKILL: Letter-Sound Relationships

Write the word *pollution* on the board and circle the word part *tion*. Write the word *pollutant* on the board and circle the word part *tant*. Pronounce each word. Which word has a *t* that sounds like /sh/? What other words do you know that have a *t* that is pronounced /sh/? What do these words have in common?

  3.b. Students know that in an environment, some kinds of plants and animals live well, some live less well, and some cannot live at all.

2 How Do People Affect Ecosystems?

People change their ecosystem. Human changes make it difficult for some other organisms to survive.

Effects on Land Ecosystems

Humans change their ecosystem as they meet their needs. People may clear a forest for farm land. Forest plants are replaced with crop plants. Forest animals are replaced by farm animals.

When people build a town or road, it becomes difficult for the local organisms to survive. Plants cannot grow in a parking lot. Trees do not grow in someone's home.

Humans clear land for resources, such as wood.

Trees are producers. They also help make the air we breathe. Cutting down trees can hurt the environment and the people and animals in it.

People can change a forest into a city. People can make a river into a lake. These changes can be helpful or harmful to the environment.

Dams can be helpful. They can stop flooding. They can bring water to dry places. They can help give water to people in cities.

Dams can also do harm. Flooding causes the soil to become rich. After dams stop flooding in an area, the land will not have as many nutrients. Dams may also make the fish populations smaller.

1. Fill in the table to tell how dams both help and harm the environment.

How Dams Are Helpful	How Dams Are Harmful
• stop _____ • bring _____ to dry places • bring water to people in _____	• prevent nutrients from being added to the _____ • can make _____ smaller

2.

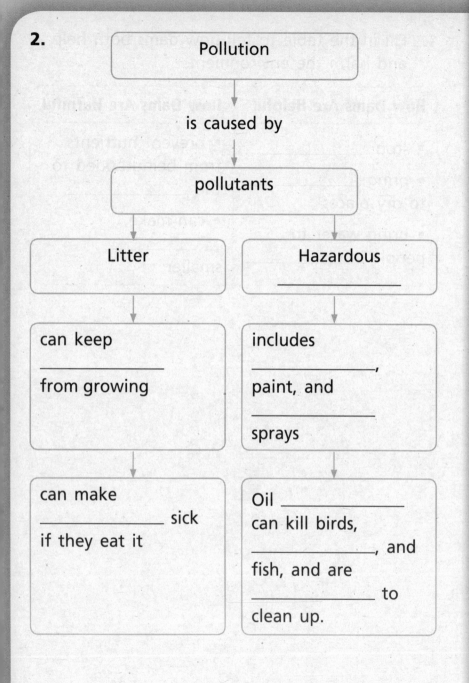

```
        Pollution
           │
           ▼
      is caused by
           │
           ▼
       pollutants
       │        │
       ▼        ▼
```

Litter	Hazardous _____
can keep _____ from growing	includes _____, paint, and _____ sprays
can make _____ sick if they eat it	Oil _____ can kill birds, _____, and fish, and are _____ to clean up.

People add things that hurt the environment. Some farmers use things to kill weeds that can get into the soil and cause pollution (puh LOO shuhn). **Pollution** is adding bad things to the environment. **Pollutants** are things that cause pollution. They can harm many organisms.

People make a lot of waste. **Litter** is trash that causes harm to an ecosystem. Most litter is garbage that people throw on the ground. Litter can harm an ecosystem. Plants cannot grow where there is a lot of litter. Animals sometimes eat litter and get sick.

Sprays can help farm crops grow, but they can also hurt other parts of the environment.

Effects on Water Ecosystems

Pollution happens when people do not throw out their waste correctly. Pollution can affect both land and water ecosystems. Some sea animals get tangled up in garbage. This can injure or kill the animals.

Hazardous (HAZ ur duhs) **waste** is waste that can pollute the environment, even in small amounts. Hazardous waste is dangerous to people and other organisms. Motor oil, paint, and insect sprays are all hazardous wastes.

Because oil is so hazardous, big spills are very dangerous for the environment. Spills normally happen when oil is being moved. Spills can harm vast ocean habitats. They can kill birds, whales, and fish. They are very difficult to clean up.

Litter can get caught on animals and harm them.

COMPARE AND CONTRAST

What is the difference between litter and hazardous waste?

Summary Like other organisms, people change the ecosystems in which they live. Human changes to an ecosystem can affect the ability of other organisms to survive in those ecosystems. Complete the diagram to tell how humans can affect a water ecosystem.

Cause	Effect
A large oil spill occurs in ocean habitats.	Ocean habitats are _____, and many _____ are killed.

Compare and Contrast What is the difference between litter and hazardous waste?

_____

_____

_____

_____

_____

_____

_____

Lesson Preview

VOCABULARY

biodegradable material Matter that breaks down easily in the environment. *(noun)*

ecotourism Travel to natural habitats that avoids harming and helps preserve these areas and the organisms that live there. *(noun)*

VOCABULARY SKILL: Prefixes

The word *biodegradable* contains the prefix *bio-* which comes from the Greek word meaning "life." What other words have you read that have this prefix?

_____

_____

 2.c. Students know decomposers recycle matter from dead plants and animals.
3.b. Students know that in an environment, some kinds of plants and animals live well, some live less well, and some cannot live at all.
3.d. Students know that most microorganisms do not cause disease and that many are helpful.

3 How Can Ecosystems Be Conserved?

We can help our ecosystem by using biodegradable materials, recycling, and practicing green agriculture.

Biodegradable Materials

Biodegradable materials are things that break down easily in the environment. Paper and wood are biodegradable materials. Things that are not biodegradable last for a long time. Some last as long as 1,000 years! Metals and most plastics are not biodegradable.

Scientists are finding ways to make more things biodegradable. There is now biodegradable plastic and biodegradable cloth.

Day 1   Day 38   Day 58

This is a new kind of plastic. It is made from plants. When it is thrown away it will break down and not pollute the environment.

Problems with Landfills

Over time a biodegradable newspaper will break down, right? It may not if the newspaper goes to a landfill.

A landfill is a large outdoor place used to bury wastes. Today, landfills are lined with plastic. They do this so no hazardous waste can leak into other ecosystems.

So, why wouldn't the newspaper break down in a landfill? It is because the garbage is packed so closely that there is little air or water. Many microorganisms that break things down cannot live there.

Landfills keep waste in relatively small areas. Limiting pollutants to small areas protects the rest of the environment from their effects. But landfills should only be used for waste that cannot be recycled, reused, or composted.

1. List two items in each category.

Item is Biodegradable	Item is Not Biodegradable
a. _____	a. _____
b. _____	b. _____

2. Tell why biodegradable items do not always decay in a landfill.

_____

_____

_____

I Wonder . . . Landfills are lined with plastic to keep hazardous waste from leaking out. What would happen if landfills were lined with a layer of wood instead of plastic?

_____

_____

_____

3. List three ways to keep biodegradable trash out of landfills.

a. _____

b. _____

c. _____

4. What are two benefits of keeping biodegradable trash out of landfills?

a. _____

b. _____

Most people do not want to have a landfill near their homes.

Another problem with landfills is their size. They are very big. And since no one wants to live near a landfill, it is hard to find a new place to put one.

The best way to make sure biodegradable trash decomposes is to keep it out of a landfill. This can be done by recycling, reusing, and composting waste. This would save a lot of space at landfills. It would also stop garbage from becoming pollution.

Preserving Rainforests

Rainforests are very important. They have many plants and animals. They also have many resources. We get medicines from rainforests. We also get fruits and oils.

Plants of the rainforest let off large amounts of oxygen. All plants and animals need oxygen to live. Plants also remove waste gases from the air. Without plants, these waste gases would cause Earth to heat up. Droughts, storms, and floods would result.

Plants of the rainforest help keep gases in Earth's air in balance.

5. List three resources that rainforests provide for people.

   a. _____

   b. _____

   c. _____

6. Rainforest plants give off _____ and remove _____ gases from the air.

7.
   Without plants to remove waste gases from air Earth would heat up. This heating would result in

   [_____]   [storms]   [_____]

8. List two reasons that people cut down rainforests.

_____

_____

_____

I Wonder . . . Ecotourism means visiting natural habitats, such as the rainforest, and helping to keep them healthy. What rules would you give to people traveling to a rainforest that would help keep the ecosystem healthy?

_____

_____

_____

_____

Ecotourists enjoy the environment without hurting it.

Many rainforests are being cut down. People do this for a few reasons. People use wood to build houses and make paper. Some use the land for farming. Others use it to raise animals.

Rainforests could be saved. The resources from the rainforest could provide money. The fruits, oils, and medicines would pay the locals more than farming or raising animals.

Ecotourism is another way to help. Ecotourism is visiting natural habitats and helping to keep them healthy. Ecotourists pay to visit rainforests and see the plants and animals. This money also helps save the forests.

Green Agriculture

You have learned some ways that farming can change an ecosystem. Forests, grasslands, and deserts can be turned into farms. Rivers and lakes are used to bring water to the farms. Some farmers use things to kill weeds that pollute the environment.

Many farmers use fertilizers on their crops. Fertilizers help plants grow. But these fertilizers can get into the water. Then the water becomes full of plants and algae. This causes fish to die.

Organic farmers do not use harmful fertilizers.

9. Fill in the diagram about fertilizers.

Farmers use fertilizers on their crops to help the plants _____.

↓

Fertilizers can get into the _____.

↓

The water becomes full of _____ and _____.

↓

Because of this, fish _____.

10. Fill in the diagram about green agriculture.

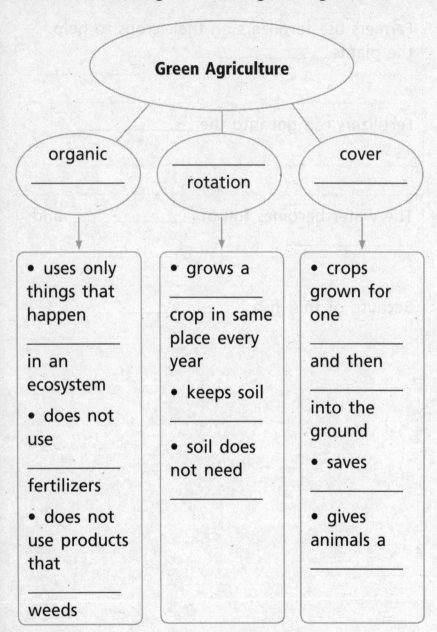

Green Agriculture

organic _____

_____ rotation

cover _____

- uses only things that happen _____ in an ecosystem
- does not use _____ fertilizers
- does not use products that _____ weeds

- grows a _____ crop in same place every year
- keeps soil _____
- soil does not need _____

- crops grown for one _____ and then _____ into the ground
- saves _____
- gives animals a _____

There are ways to farm that do not hurt the environment. This is called green agriculture. Green agriculture helps save water, improve soil, and keep the ecosystem safe.

One kind of green agriculture is organic farming. Organic farming only uses things that happen naturally in an ecosystem. They do not use harmful fertilizers or products that kill weeds.

Another kind of green agriculture is crop rotation. Crop rotation means that a farmer grows a different crop in the same place every year. Without crop rotation, the soil loses its nutrients. This makes it so the farmer has to use fertilizer. When the farmer rotates crops, the soil stays rich and fertilizer is not needed.

Green agriculture also includes growing cover crops. These are crops that are grown for a year and then mixed into the ground. This makes the soil rich. It saves water. And it gives animals a habitat.

Zero Waste

The goal of zero waste is to recycle and reuse items so that very little new waste is made. This keeps waste out of landfills. It keeps waste from causing pollution. Reaching this goal can also save ecosystems. If shoppers carried their groceries home in a cloth bag, fewer paper bags would be needed. Not as many trees would have to be cut down for the paper. Forests would be saved.

Recycling helps save minerals, metals, and oils. Glass, paper, and plastics are some of the things that can be recycled. Many things can be made from recycled goods, including clothing, newspapers, and furniture.

This is a paper recycling center in San José, California.

Summary Some ways ecosystems can be conserved include using biodegradable materials, recycling, and practicing green agriculture.

How does zero waste help save ecosystems?

_____

_____

_____

_____

 Problem and Solution What is one way that rainforests can be preserved?

Problem	Solution
Rainforests are being cut down.	

PROBLEM AND SOLUTION

What is one way that rainforests can be preserved?

95

Write a short paragraph using the words on the page.

biodegradable material (by oh dee GRAYD ah buhl muh TEER ee uhl) Matter that breaks down easily in the environment.

material biodegradable Material que se descompone con facilidad en el medio ambiente.

compost (KAHM pohst) Decayed material from once-living things that is used to enrich the soil.

abono orgánico Material de desecho de lo que fueron seres vivos, que se usa para enriquecer la tierra.

decay (dih KAY) To break down into simpler materials.

descomponerse Separarse en materiales más simples.

decomposer (dee kuhm POH zur) A living thing that breaks down the remains of dead organisms.

desintegrador Ser vivo que descompone los restos de los organismos muertos.

ecotourism (ee koh TOOR ihx uhm) Travel to natural habitats that avoids harming and helps preserve these areas and the organisms that live there.

ecoturismo Viajes por los hábitat naturales, en los que se evitan los daños y se ayuda a preservar estas zonas y a los organismos que viven en ellas.

Glossary

hazardous waste (HAZ ur duhs WAYST) Waste that can pollute the environment even when it occurs in very small amounts.

desechos peligrosos Desechos que incluso en pequeñas cantidades pueden contaminar el medio ambiente.

litter (lih TUR) Trash that is not disposed of in a way that prevents harm to ecosystems.

basura Desechos que se tiran sin prevenir daños al ecosistema.

nutrient recycling (noo TREE uhnt ree SY kuhl ihng) The process of breaking down materials into a different form that can be used again.

reciclaje de nutrientes Proceso que sirve para descomponer materiales de forma que se puedan usar de nuevo.

pollutant (pah LOOT uhnt) A material that causes pollution.

contaminante Material que produce contaminación.

pollution (pah LOO shun) The addition of harmful materials to the environment.

contaminación La liberación de materiales perjudiciales en el medio ambiente.

scavenger (SKAV uhn jur) An animal that feeds on the remains or wastes of dead animals.

carroñero Animal que se alimenta de los restos o desechos de animales muertos.

 Visit www.eduplace.com to play puzzles and word games.

(Circle) the English words and their meaning for three glossary words.

Chapter Review

WHAT DID YOU LEARN?

Vocabulary

❶ Circle the correct answer on the page.

Comprehension

❷ _____

❸ _____

❹ _____

Critical Thinking

❺ _____

_____

_____

_____

Think About What You Have Read

Vocabulary

❶ An animal that feeds on the remains of dead animals is a/an _____.

  A) pollutant

  B) decomposer

  C) scavenger

  D) compost

Comprehension

❷ Trash that is thrown on the ground or in water is _____.

❸ One way to keep material out of landfills is to _____.

❹ How can compost improve soil?

Critical Thinking

❺ How are scavengers and decomposers alike and different?

KWL

WHAT DO YOU KNOW?

Write one thing you know about each of the topics listed.

a. Properties of minerals: _____

_____

_____

b. How minerals are identified: _____

_____

_____

c. How rocks form: _____

_____

_____

d. The rock cycle: _____

_____

_____

Rocks and Minerals

Contents

1 What Are the Properties of Minerals? . . 102

2 How Are Minerals Identified? 107

3 How Do Rocks Differ? 110

4 What Is the Rock Cycle? 114

Glossary 116

KWL

WHAT DO YOU WANT TO KNOW?

Skim the pictures and headings in this chapter. Write one question that you have about each of these topics.

a. Properties of minerals: _____

_____

_____

b. Identifying minerals: _____

_____

_____

c. How rocks form: _____

_____

_____

d. The rock cycle: _____

_____

_____

Lesson Preview

VOCABULARY

cleavage The tendency of a mineral to split easily along flat surfaces. *(noun)*

hardness A measure of how easily a mineral can be scratched. *(noun)*

luster The way a mineral shines, or reflects light. *(noun)*

mineral A nonliving solid material that has a definite chemical makeup and is found in Earth's outermost layer. *(noun)*

streak The color of a mineral when it is ground to a powder. *(noun)*

VOCABULARY SKILL: Prefixes and Suffixes

The word *hardness* contains the suffix *-ness*, which means "a state or condition." Use your knowledge of the word *hard* to write your own definition of *hardness*.

_____

_____

  4.b. Students know how to identify common minerals by using a table of mineral properties.

1 What Are the Properties of Minerals?

Minerals can be described by their luster, color, streak, hardness, and cleavage.

Luster

A **mineral** (MIHN ur uhl) is a nonliving solid found in nature. Minerals are found in the earth. They have many uses. Windows are made from minerals. So are pipes, wires, and parts of buildings. A mineral's properties make it useful. A property is a way something can be described.

One property of a mineral is its luster. **Luster** describes how shiny a mineral is. Some minerals, such as pyrite, are shiny like gold and silver. Others, such as gypsum, are dull.

fluorite

silver

The luster of a mineral is a clue to its identity. The mineral can be shiny like silver or have a glassy luster like fluorite.

Color and Streak

Another property of a mineral is its color. Color is an easy way to describe a mineral, but it is not the best way. Colors of minerals can change.

If you rub a rock against something hard, it will turn to powder. The color of the mineral when it becomes a powder is called the **streak**. For some minerals, the streak is the same as the color. But some minerals have different streaks and colors. Streak is a good way to identify these minerals.

pink beryl

blue beryl

green beryl

The color of the mineral beryl can change, depending on the sample.

1. List three uses of minerals.

   a. _____

   b. _____

   c. _____

2. Look at the minerals on these pages. Circle the mineral that has a shiny luster.

3. How is the streak of a mineral related to its color?

   _____

   _____

   _____

4. The hardness of a mineral is a measure of how easy it is to scratch the mineral. What can you use to test a mineral's hardness?

a. _____

b. _____

c. _____

5. Use the Mohs scale to find the hardness of the following minerals or other materials.

a. calcite _____

b. glass _____

c. quartz _____

d. topaz _____

e. diamond _____

Mohs Hardness Scale

Photo	Mineral	Hardness
	talc	1
	gypsum	2
	fingernail	2.5
	calcite	3
	copper penny	3.2
	fluorite	4
	apatite	5
	glass	5.5
	feldspar	6
	steel file	6.5
	quartz	7
	topaz	8
	corundum	9
	diamond	10

Hardness

The **hardness** of a mineral is a measure of how easy it is to scratch it. You can test for hardness using items like fingernails, pennies, or nails.

Another way to test the hardness is to compare a mineral to the Mohs scale. Ten minerals are listed on the scale. They are listed from softest to hardest. Look at the Mohs scale to the left to see how minerals compare.

The Mohs scale lists the hardness of ten common minerals.

Cleavage

Another mineral property is cleavage. **Cleavage** is when a mineral splits along flat surfaces. The flat surfaces are called cleavage planes.

Mica, a mineral, has cleavage planes that are all in the same direction. It splits into thin sheets. Halite, another mineral, splits along three planes. When it splits it makes pieces shaped like cubes. Some stones, such as diamonds and rubies, do not split. To shape them, they must be ground. They make very shiny surfaces when they are ground. These are called facets. The number of facets give gemstones different looks. One popular gem cut has 57 facets.

Cleavage

Mica

Calcite

Ruby

These minerals cleave in different ways.

6. Cleavage is a mineral property. A mineral has cleavage when it _____ along flat surfaces.

7. Complete the chart to describe the cleavage of some minerals.

Mineral	Cleavage Description
Mica	Its planes are all in the _____ direction. It splits into _____ sheets.
Halite	It splits along _____ planes. It forms pieces shaped like _____.
Diamonds and rubies	These minerals do not split; they must be _____ to make shiny surfaces called _____.

Summary Minerals can be described according to a set of properties that include luster, color, streak, hardness, and cleavage. Minerals are used to make many things. List how three different minerals are used by the baseball player shown on this page.

a. _____

_____

b. _____

_____

c. _____

_____

Main Idea What are some of the properties of minerals?

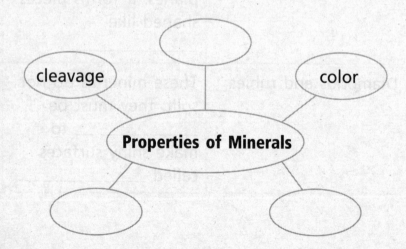

Using Mineral Properties

You have learned some ways that minerals are used. Now read about the ways minerals are helpful to this baseball player.

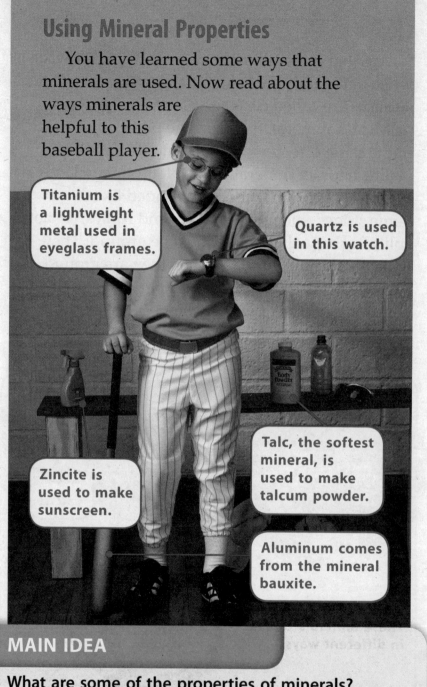

Titanium is a lightweight metal used in eyeglass frames.

Quartz is used in this watch.

Zincite is used to make sunscreen.

Talc, the softest mineral, is used to make talcum powder.

Aluminum comes from the mineral bauxite.

MAIN IDEA

What are some of the properties of minerals?

How Are Minerals Identified?

You can run tests to find a mineral's properties. Compare the outcome to a table of properties.

Nonmetallic Minerals

Look at the Properties of Minerals table on page 9. It is divided into metallic and nonmetallic minerals. A **nonmetallic mineral** looks dull. You can use the table to name an unknown mineral. To identify a mineral, try these tests:

- **LUSTER** How shiny is the mineral?
- **HARDNESS** What scratches it?
- **COLOR** What color is it?
- **CLEAVAGE** Does it divide along a flat surface?
- **OTHER PROPERTIES** Does it have any strange properties?

luster

hardness

cleavage

streak

other properties

VOCABULARY

metallic mineral A mineral that is shiny like metal. *(noun)*

nonmetallic mineral A mineral that is dull or glassy. *(noun)*

VOCABULARY SKILL: Antonyms

Antonyms are words that have opposite meanings. *Dull* and *shiny* are antonyms used to describe a mineral's luster. Use each word in a sentence.

_____

_____

_____

_____

4.b. Students know how to identify common minerals by using a table of mineral properties.

Compare and contrast the properties used to identify nonmetallic and metallic minerals. Use the Properties of Minerals table on page 109 to help you.

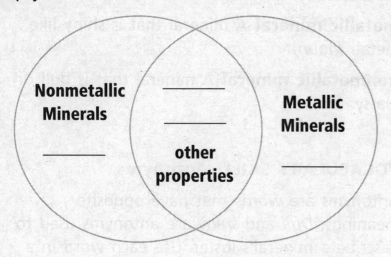

Nonmetallic Minerals

————

————

————

other properties

Metallic Minerals

————

I Wonder . . . Hardness can be determined by trying to scratch a mineral with another mineral. One of the materials used to determine hardness on the chart on page 109 is a fingernail. How could a fingernail be made of "minerals"?

——————————————————————

——————————————————————

——————————————————————

——————————————————————

Metallic Minerals

A **metallic mineral** is one that is shiny like a metal. Luster will tell if the mineral is metallic or nonmetallic. Then you can test it for hardness. What if the mineral you want to test is metallic? What if it can scratch glass? What other properties should you test for?

- **COLOR** Check your mineral's color with those in the chart. See if there is a match.
- **STREAK** What color is the mineral's streak? Find the mineral on the chart that has the same color streak as yours.
- **OTHER PROPERTIES** Does the mineral have special properties? What if you test the mineral and find that it is magnetic? Magnetic means that it pulls some other metals toward it. Which mineral in the table is magnetic?

nonmetallic

metallic

Properties of Minerals					
Luster	Hardness	Color	Cleavage	Other	Name
Nonmetallic	C	colorless, white	yes; parallelograms	bubbles when acid is placed on it	Calcite
Nonmetallic	G	colorless, beige, pink	yes	hardness very close to glass	Feldspar
Nonmetallic	F	colorless, white	yes	tastes salty	Halite
Nonmetallic	G	dark green to black	yes; diamond shape	splits easily	Hornblende
Nonmetallic	F	dark brown, black, or silver-white	yes	flakes when peeled	Mica
Nonmetallic	G	colorless, white, rose, smoky, purple, brown	no	looks glassy, chips like glass	Quartz
Nonmetallic	F	white, greenish to gray	yes	usually flaky	Talc
Luster	Hardness	Color	Streak	Other	Name
Metallic	C	gray	gray to black	heavy for its size	Galena
Metallic	F	yellow	golden yellow	used for jewelry	Gold
Metallic	G	steel gray	reddish	may have reddish patches	Hematite
Metallic	G	black	black	magnetic	Magnetite
Metallic	G	brassy yellow	greenish black	looks like gold	Pyrite

Key: F = scratched by fingernail; C = scratched by copper penny; G = scratches glass

CLASSIFY

What test is used to classify a mineral as metallic or nonmetallic?

Summary The properties of a mineral can be learned by observing and by doing a series of tests. Then, by comparing its properties with those listed in a table of mineral properties, the mineral can be identified.

Complete the diagram to show how to classify a mineral by its luster.

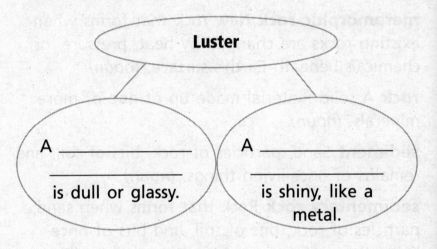

Luster

A _____ _____ is dull or glassy.

A _____ _____ is shiny, like a metal.

Classify What test is used to classify a mineral as metallic or nonmetallic?

_____

109

Lesson Preview

VOCABULARY

igneous rock Rock that forms when melted, or molten, rock from deep below Earth's surface cools and hardens. *(noun)*

metamorphic rock New rock that forms when existing rocks are changed by heat, pressure, or chemicals beneath Earth's surface. *(noun)*

rock A solid material made up of one or more minerals. *(noun)*

sediment Sand, particles of rock, bits of soil, and remains of once-living things. *(noun)*

sedimentary rock Rock that forms when sand, particles of rock, bits of soil, and bits of once-living things are pressed together and harden. *(noun)*

  4.a. Students know how to tell the difference between igneous, sedimentary, and metamorphic rocks by their properties and ways they formed (the rock cycle).

3 How Do Rocks Differ?

Three kinds of rock make up Earth's crust: igneous, sedimentary, and metamorphic.

Earth's Layers

Earth is made up of layers, or sheets. The outer layer is the crust. The ocean floor is part of the crust. So are the large pieces of land, called continents (KAHN tuh nuhnts). The crust is the thinnest layer of Earth. It is made up of rock. **Rock** is made of minerals.

The next layer down is the mantle (MAN tuhl). It is thick rock. The lower part of the mantle is hard. The upper part has soft rock.

The inner layer of Earth is the core (kawr). The core is a tight ball. It has a soft outside and a hard inside. The inside is the hottest part of Earth.

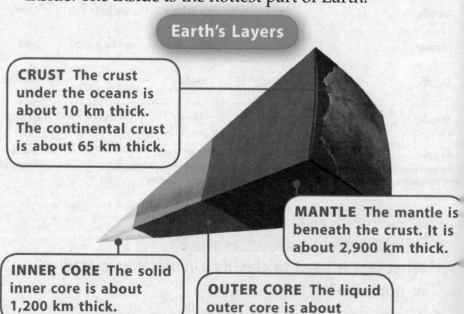

Earth's Layers

CRUST The crust under the oceans is about 10 km thick. The continental crust is about 65 km thick.

MANTLE The mantle is beneath the crust. It is about 2,900 km thick.

INNER CORE The solid inner core is about 1,200 km thick.

OUTER CORE The liquid outer core is about 2,250 km thick.

Igneous Rock

Three kinds of rock make up Earth's crust. **Igneous** (IHG nee uhs) **rock** forms when melted, or molten, rock from deep in Earth cools and gets hard. Molten rock has different minerals. As the rock gets hard, these minerals become crystals (KRIHS tuhlz). A diamond is a crystal.

An opening in the crust is a volcano (vahl KAY noh). Sometimes molten rock will come out of a volcano. This rock cools very fast. The crystals in this rock are very small, or there are none at all. Large crystals are found in the rocks that cool slowly under the crust.

Molten rock hardens to form igneous rock.

Igneous Rock

Obsidian (ahb SIHD ee uhn) is formed when molten rock cools quickly.

Basalt (buh SAWLT) makes up much of Earth's crust beneath the oceans.

Granite (GRAN iht) is molten rock that hardens in the crust.

1. List Earth's layers and their thicknesses.

   a. _____

   b. _____

   c. _____

   d. _____

2. How does igneous rock form?

   _____

   _____

3. Use the clues to identify each type of igneous rock.

   a. This igneous rock makes up much of Earth's crust beneath the oceans.

      _____

   b. When molten rock cools quickly, this igneous rock forms. _____

   c. This igneous rock forms when molten rock hardens in Earth's crust. _____

111

4. Complete the diagram to tell how sedimentary rock forms.

| Rock is broken into sediment when _____ occurs. | → | Layers of sediment settle _____ of each other. Layers of sediment grow very thick. | → | The weight on the bottom becomes _____. Minerals _____ the rock together. |

5. Rocks changed by heat or pressure under Earth's surface are metamorphic rocks. Complete the diagrams below to tell how rocks change.

Metamorphic Rock

| **a.** Limestone (sedimentary rock) | → | _____ |

| **b.** Granite (igneous rock) | → | _____ |

Sedimentary Rock

Sand, bits of rock and soil, and the remains of dead organisms are called **sediment** (SEHD uh muhnt). **Sedimentary** (sehd uh MEHN tuh ree) **rock** is rock that is made when pieces of sediment come together and get hard. Rock is broken into sediment during weathering. Weathering is when sediment is moved by wind, water, and ice. Over time, layers of sediment settle on top of each other.

As the layers grow, the weight on the bottom gets very heavy. Over millions of years, the bottom layers become rock. Minerals fill in any holes in the rock. Then they cement, or glue, all of it together.

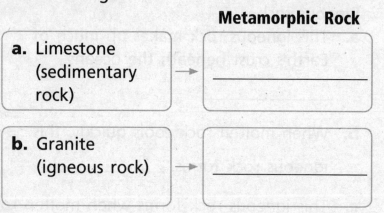

Bits of sand, rocks, and once-living things settle and pack together.

Sedimentary Rock

Conglomerate (kuhn GLAHM ur iht) is formed from sediments of different sizes.

Limestone sometimes forms when the remains of ocean animals become cemented together.

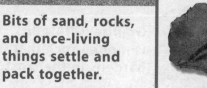
Shale is formed from thin outer layers of clay. Shale is smooth and breaks easily into layers.

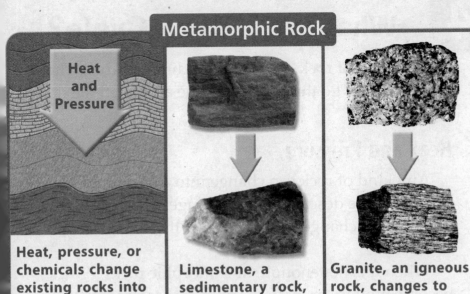

Metamorphic Rock

Heat, pressure, or chemicals change existing rocks into metamorphic rocks.

Limestone, a sedimentary rock, changes to marble.

Granite, an igneous rock, changes to gneiss (nys).

Metamorphic Rock

Metamorphic (meht uh MAWR fihk) **rock** is rock that is made when old rocks are changed by heat or pressure under Earth's surface. Both igneous and sedimentary rock can be changed into metamorphic rock. Old metamorphic rock can also be changed to new metamorphic rock.

How do these rocks change? Inside the earth, rocks are being pushed very hard. This makes heat build up. This heat and pushing makes the rocks change.

COMPARE AND CONTRAST

Contrast how large crystals and how small crystals form in igneous rock.

Summary Three basic kinds of rock—igneous, sedimentary, and metamorphic—make up Earth's crust. Each kind of rock forms in a different way and has different traits. Complete the diagram about the three basic kinds of rock.

Rock: A solid made up of one or more _____.

| When sediment is cemented together and gets hard, it forms _____ _____. | When existing rocks are changed by heat, pressure, or chemicals they form _____ _____. | When melted rock cools and hardens it forms _____ _____. |

Compare and Contrast Contrast how large crystals and how small crystals form in igneous rock.

_____

_____

_____

VOCABULARY

rock cycle The continuous series of changes that rocks undergo. (*noun*)

VOCABULARY SKILL: Sentence context

By reading a sentence or a paragraph, or by studying the pages around it, you can often find the definition of a word. Look at the Rock Cycle diagram on page 115. Find the label for *weathering* that connects a metamorphic rock to sediments. Based on this information, what can you infer about weathering?

_____

_____

4.a. Students know how to tell the difference between igneous, sedimentary, and metamorphic rocks by their properties and ways they formed (the rock cycle).

4 What Is the Rock Cycle?

Any kind of rock can become a different rock. The changes rocks go through over time are called the rock cycle.

Heat and Pressure

Any kind of rock can change into a different kind. The **rock cycle** describes these changes. This cycle shows what changes rock and how the changes are made.

When it is hot enough, metamorphic rocks become molten, or melted. When this rock cools and gets hard, it is igneous rock. This example is shown on page 15 in the rock cycle diagram. Examples of how other rocks can change are also shown.

marble

Marble is a metamorphic rock. It is used to build things. It is removed from the ground in a quarry.

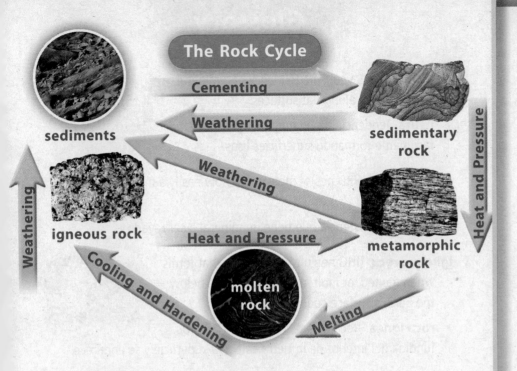

The Rock Cycle

sediments

Cementing

Weathering

sedimentary rock

Weathering

Heat and Pressure

igneous rock

Weathering

Heat and Pressure

metamorphic rock

Cooling and Hardening

molten rock

Melting

Weathering and Cementing

Rocks change through weathering. Weathering is the breaking down of rock. It happens when wind, water, or ice break rock into sediment. Weathering takes a long time.

Cementing changes sediment into sedimentary rock. Over time, layers of sediment build up. The weight from above changes the lower layers into rock. Minerals fill in the cracks of the rock. This cements, or glues, the sediment together.

SEQUENCE

Use the rock cycle diagram to explain how metamorphic rock changes into sedimentary rock.

Summary Any type of rock—metamorphic, igneous, or sedimentary—can change into any other type of rock. The continuous series of changes that rocks undergo is called the rock cycle.

Use the words *Weathering* or *Cementing* to correctly complete each sentence below.

a. _____ breaks down rock.

b. _____ changes sediment into sedimentary rock.

c. _____ occurs when wind, water, or ice break rock into sediment.

d. _____ cements or glues sediment together.

Sequence Use the rock cycle diagram to explain how metamorphic rock changes into sedimentary rock.

_____

_____

_____

Unscramble these words to make terms that are about rocks.

usigeno _____

lacmitle _____

sturel _____

nearlim _____

cleavage (KLEE vedj) The tendency of a mineral to split easily along flat surfaces.

fisura Tendencia de un mineral a partirse fácilmente formando superficies lisas.

hardness (HAWRD nes) A measure of how easily a mineral can be scratched.

dureza Resistencia que tiene un mineral a ser rayado.

igneous rock (IHG nee uhs rawk) Rock that forms when melted, or molten, rock from deep below the Earth's surface cools and hardens.

roca ígnea Roca que se forma cuando la roca fundida del interior de la Tierra sale a la superficie y se endurece.

luster (LUH stehr) The way a mineral shines, or reflects light.

brillo Luz que emite o refleja un mineral.

metallic mineral (MEH tahl ihk MIHN ur uhl) A mineral that is shiny like metal.

mineral metálico Mineral que brilla como el metal.

metamorphic rock (meht uh MAWR fihk rawk) New rock that forms when existing rocks are changed by heat, pressure, or chemicals beneath Earth's surface.

roca metamórfica Roca nueva que se forma cuando las rocas ya existentes son modificadas por el calor, la presión o los compuestos químicos bajo la superficie de la Tierra.

Glossary

mineral (MIHN ur uhl) A nonliving solid material that has a definite chemical makeup and is found in Earth's outermost layer.

mineral Material sólido sin vida que tiene una composición química definida y se encuentra en la capa exterior de la Tierra.

nonmetallic mineral (NOHN meh tahl ihk MIHN ur uhl) A mineral that is dull or glassy.

mineral no metálico Mineral que es opaco o vidrioso.

rock (rawk) A solid material made up of one or more minerals.

roca Material sólido que está compuesto de uno o más minerales.

rock cycle (rawk SY kuhl) The continuous series of changes that rocks undergo.

ciclo de las rocas Serie continua de cambios producidos en las rocas.

sediment (SEHD uh muhnt) Sand, particles of rock, bits of soil, and remains of once-living things.

sedimento Arena, partículas de roca, trocitos de suelo y restos de lo que fueron seres vivos.

sedimentary rock (sehd uh MEHN tuh ree rawk) Rock that forms when sand, particles of rock, bits of soil, and bits of once-living things are pressed together and harden.

roca sedimentaria Roca que se forma cuando arena, partículas de roca y restos de seres vivos se compactan y endurecen.

streak (streek) The color of a mineral when it is ground to a powder.

raspadura El color de un mineral cuando se muele hasta convertirlo en polvo.

Visit www.eduplace.com to play puzzles and word games.

Circle the words in the Glossary that are the same in English and Spanish.

Chapter Review

WHAT DID YOU LEARN?

Vocabulary

❶ (Circle) the correct answer on the page.

Comprehension

❷ _____
_____

❸ _____
_____

❹ _____
_____
_____
_____

Critical Thinking

❺ _____
_____
_____

Responding

Think About What You Have Read

Vocabulary

❶ The way a mineral shines is called its _____.

A) sediment

B) streak

C) luster

D) mineral

Comprehension

❷ A mineral that is dull is called a/an _____.

❸ Sand, bits of rock, and the remains of organisms are called _____.

❹ How can you use a table of mineral properties to identify a mineral?

Critical Thinking

❺ In the rock cycle, what must occur for igneous rock to become sedimentary rock?

WHAT DO YOU KNOW?

Write something you know about each of the causes of rapid changes on Earth that are listed below:

Earthquakes _____

_____

_____

Volcanoes _____

_____

_____

Landslides _____

_____

_____

Rapid Changes on Earth

Contents

1 What Are Earthquakes? 122

2 What Are Volcanoes? 128

3 What Are Landslides? 131

Glossary 135

WHAT DO YOU WANT TO KNOW?

Skim the pictures and headings in this chapter. List one thing you want to know about each of these causes of rapid changes on Earth:

a. Earthquakes _____

_____

_____

b. Volcanoes _____

_____

_____

c. Landslides _____

_____

VOCABULARY

creep Slow movement of land along a fault. *(noun)*

earthquake A sudden movement of part of Earth's crust. *(noun)*

epicenter Where an earthquake is felt most strongly or has its greatest intensity. *(noun)*

fault A crack in Earth's crust. *(noun)*

focus The point underground where an earthquake starts. *(noun)*

seismology The study of earthquakes. *(noun)*

tsunami A very large ocean wave caused by an earthquake that occurs on the ocean floor. *(noun)*

VOCABULARY SKILL: Compound Words

Earthquake is made up of two smaller words. *Earth* refers to our planet. *Quake* means to "shake." Write your own definition of *earthquake*.

_____

_____

_____

5.a. Students know changes in the earth are caused by slow processes, such as erosion, and by rapid processes, such as landslides, volcanic eruptions, and earthquakes.

1 What Are Earthquakes?

Earth's surface is always changing. Earthquakes cause quick changes to the surface.

Faults

Suppose you are standing in a field. A friend is with you. Suddenly, the ground starts to shake. The land you are standing on moves up. The shaking stops. You look at your friend. He is standing in the same spot, but now he is far below you. An earthquake (URTH kwayk) has just happened. An **earthquake** is the sudden movement of part of Earth's crust.

Earthquakes happen when parts of the crust hit, move apart, or slide past each other. This happens along a **fault** (fawlt), or crack, in Earth's crust.

Along the San Andreas Fault, huge pieces of Earth's crust press against one another. Earthquakes are common along this fault line.

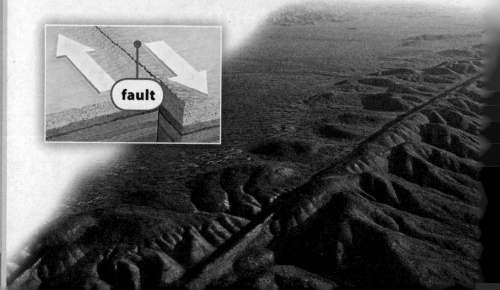

fault

Large Faults in California

— fault

≡ part of fault in which creep occurs

San Francisco
Hollister
San Andreas Fault
Parkfield
Wrightwood
San Bernardino
Los Angeles

The San Andreas Fault is a well-known fault. It runs from northern California all the way down to San Bernardino. This fault is over 1,200 km long and as deep as 16 km. Some of the strongest earthquakes in the United States have happened along this fault.

Slow movements happen all the time along faults. This is called **creep**. For over 25 years, scientists have measured the creep along the San Andreas Fault in Hollister, California. In one place, the creep has been about a half an inch a year.

1. a. What is a fault? What happens along faults?

_____

_____

b. Circle the fault line in the photo on page 122. Put an X on the fault in the drawing on that page.

2. Creep is a slow movement along a fault.

a. Look at the map. Which cities mark the beginning and end of creep found on the San Andreas Fault?

_____

_____

b. On the map, circle the name of the place along the San Andreas Fault where scientists have measured creep for the past 25 years.

3. What causes an earthquake?

_____

_____

_____

_____

_____

_____

_____

4. Look at the map. List three places where the 1906 San Francisco earthquake was the most intense.

a. _____

b. _____

c. _____

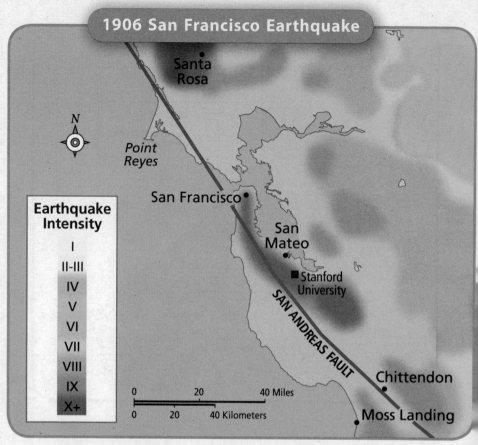

1906 San Francisco Earthquake

Santa Rosa

N

Point Reyes

San Francisco

San Mateo

Stanford University

SAN ANDREAS FAULT

Chittendon

Moss Landing

Earthquake Intensity

I
II-III
IV
V
VI
VII
VIII
IX
X+

0   20   40 Miles

0   20   40 Kilometers

In 1906, an earthquake and fire destroyed San Francisco.

Causes of Earthquakes

Earth's crust is always changing. Layers of rock deep down push up against the upper levels. This pushing, or pressure, can build up over a very long time. As this pressure builds, the crust on the surface moves so slowly that it cannot be seen.

Sometimes the pressure building up below the surface becomes too strong. Then the land on one or both sides of a fault may move suddenly. This sudden movement is an earthquake.

When an earthquake happens on the ocean floor, it may cause a tsunami (tsoo NAH mee). A **tsunami** is a huge wave. Strong earthquakes can cause tsunamis, which can do great damage on land.

What you will feel in an earthquake depends on how far you are from the focus (FO kus). The **focus** is the place underground where the earthquake starts.

Energy moves away from the focus in waves. The point on the surface that is right above the focus is called the epicenter (EHP ih sehn tur). The **epicenter** is where an earthquake is strongest.

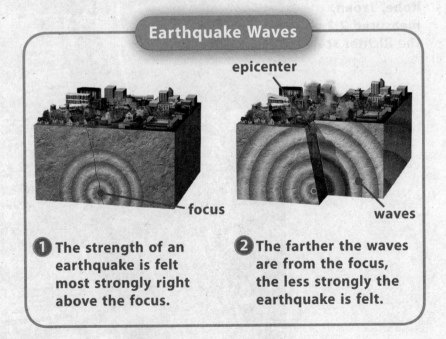

Earthquake Waves

epicenter

focus

waves

1 The strength of an earthquake is felt most strongly right above the focus.

2 The farther the waves are from the focus, the less strongly the earthquake is felt.

5. Where would an earthquake need to occur to cause a tsunami?

_____

6. What is the difference between the focus of an earthquake and the epicenter of an earthquake?

_____

_____

_____

7. Where is an earthquake the strongest?

_____

8. The study of earthquakes is called

_____.

9. The amount of energy an earthquake has is

its _____.

10. Scientists measure the amount of energy of

an earthquake on the _____ scale.

11. List two ways to stay safe during an
earthquake.

a. _____

_____

_____

b. _____

_____

_____

The study of earthquakes is called **seismology** (syz MAHL uh jee). Seismologists measure an earthquake's energy. The amount of energy is called the magnitude. It is measured on the Richter scale. An earthquake that measures 3.5 or less on the scale may not be felt. One that measures 7.5 is a major earthquake that can cause much damage to an area.

Big earthquakes can move rock on the surface and build new landforms, such as hills or mountains. Over time, mountains can be pushed up and valleys can be made. New faults might be made, too.

In 1995 an earthquake in Kobe, Japan, measured 7.2 on the Richter scale.

Earthquake-Safe Design

Earthquakes can be dangerous. Strong earthquakes can knock over buildings and kill people.

Buildings can be built so they do not fall during an earthquake. Some materials, such as wood and steel, can bend. They are good to use.

Earthquake Safety
Here are some guidelines for staying safe during and after an earthquake.
Know how to telephone the police and fire departments.
In case of a gas leak, do not turn lights on or off. Do not use candles or matches.
Know which radio station to tune to.
If you are indoors, stay indoors. Take cover near an inside wall and under a sturdy desk or table. Stay there until the shaking stops.
If you are outdoors, find an open area away from buildings and power lines. Crouch down and cover your head.
If you are in a car, stay there with your seatbelt fastened.
When the shaking stops, take these steps.
Listen to the radio for the latest emergency information.
Use the telephone only to report life-threatening emergencies.

MAIN IDEA

What effect can a violent earthquake have on Earth's surface?

Summary Earth's surface is constantly changing. Earthquakes cause rapid changes to Earth's surface. Complete the sentences to tell about earthquakes.

Earthquakes occur when sections of the crust come together, move apart, or ______________ each other.

Movements of the crust usually take place along a ______________, or crack, in Earth's crust.

Look at the picture below. Label the fault. Then describe the movement of the sections of Earth's crust shown.

____

____

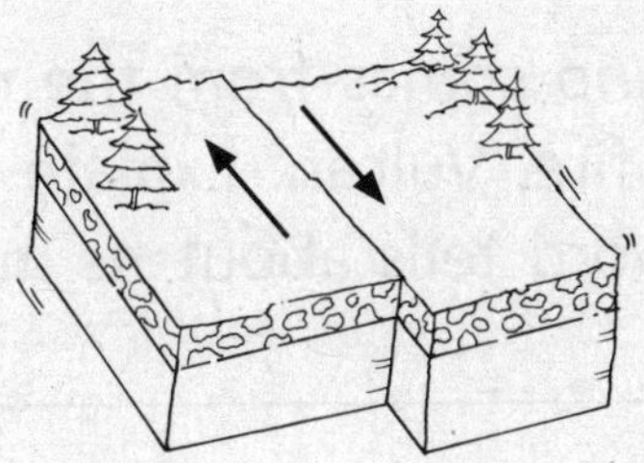

Main Idea What effect can a violent earthquake have on Earth's surface?

____

____

____

VOCABULARY

lava Molten rock that reaches Earth's surface. *(noun)*

magma The molten rock beneath Earth's surface. *(noun)*

volcano An opening in Earth's crust through which hot ash, gases, and molten rock escape from deep within Earth. *(noun)*

VOCABULARY SKILL: Word Origins

The word *volcano* comes from the name for the Roman god of fire, Vulcan. Explain what the origin of the word tells about its meaning.

_____

_____

_____

_____

2 What Are Volcanoes?

A volcano erupts when pressure forces hot rock through a crack in Earth's crust. Volcanoes change the surface of Earth.

How Volcanoes Erupt

A **volcano** (vahl KAY noh) is an opening in Earth's crust. Through this opening hot ash, gases, and melted rock from deep within Earth reach the surface. Melted rock below Earth's surface is **magma** (MAG muh). Melted rock above the surface is **lava** (LAH vuh).

Deep beneath Earth's surface, it is very hot. It is so hot that rock melts. As magma rises to the surface, some gets hard and becomes igneous rock. But pressure pushes some through Earth quickly. This rock reaches the surface as lava.

Volcanoes erupt differently. Some release thick lava slowly from their openings. Others spit lava, ash, and gases high into the air. Any volcano that erupts can change Earth's surface.

5.a. Students know changes in the earth are caused by slow processes, such as erosion, and by rapid processes, such as landslides, volcanic eruptions, and earthquakes.

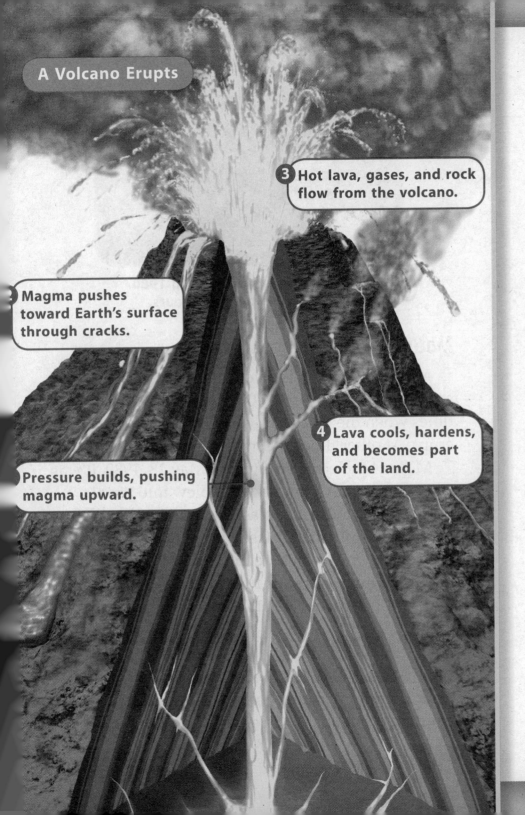

A Volcano Erupts

3 Hot lava, gases, and rock flow from the volcano.

Magma pushes toward Earth's surface through cracks.

4 Lava cools, hardens, and becomes part of the land.

Pressure builds, pushing magma upward.

Complete the diagram to show how a volcano erupts.

How a Volcano Erupts

Inside a volcano, pressure builds. The pressure pushes _____ upward.

Magma pushes toward Earth's _____ through _____.

Hot _____, gases, and _____ flow from the volcano.

Lava _____, hardens, and becomes part of the _____.

I Wonder . . . Earthquakes and volcanoes often occur in the same areas. Why might this be?

_____

_____

_____

_____

Summary A volcano erupts when pressure pushes molten rock up through cracks in Earth's crust onto the surface. Volcanoes change Earth's surface. Describe two ways that volcanoes erupt.

a. _____

_____

b. _____

_____

Cause and Effect What changes occurred to Earth as a result of the eruption of Mount St. Helens?

Cause	Effect
Mount St. Helens erupted.	_____ _____ _____ _____ _____

Mount St. Helens erupted in 1980. The eruption lasted nine hours.

Mount St. Helens

Mount St. Helens is a volcano in Washington state. It has existed for 40,000 years. There were times when the volcano was active and able to erupt. At other times the mountain was quiet.

Mount St. Helens erupted on May 18, 1980. It was a big eruption. Ash and hot gas blew into the air. Rocks, mud, and water crashed onto the side of the mountain. More than 380 sq km of forest were destroyed. One side of the mountain was blown off. This left a huge crater, or hole, in the earth. Ash from the eruption reached 11 other states.

CAUSE AND EFFECT

What changes occurred to Earth as a result of the eruption of Mount St. Helens?

130

What Are Landslides?

3

Landslides cause quick changes to Earth's surface. There are many causes of landslides. Heavy rain, melting snow, earthquakes, and volcanoes can all cause a landslide.

Causes and Effects

When Mount St. Helens erupted, it caused a landslide. A **landslide** is when loose rock and soil move suddenly down a hill. Mudslides and rockslides are kinds of landslides.

Earthquakes and eruptions can cause landslides. Soil and rock get loose in the shaking. Then they will slide downhill. The steeper the hill, the faster soil and rock slide down.

These vehicles were buried in a mudslide.

VOCABULARY

landslide The sudden movement of loose rock and soil down a steep slope. *(noun)*

VOCABULARY SKILL: Similar Words

Read the definition of *landslide*. Tell what you think mudslides and rockslides are.

_____

_____

_____

5.a. Students know changes in the earth are caused by slow processes, such as erosion, and by rapid processes, such as landslides, volcanic eruptions, and earthquakes.

131

1. List five possible causes of landslides in hilly places.

   a. _____

   b. _____

   c. _____

   d. _____

   e. _____

2. How can wildfires cause landslides?

   _____

   _____

   _____

   _____

   _____

Some landslides are caused by rain. Some are caused by melting snow. These happen in hilly places.

Wildfires can cause landslides. Fire often destroys all the plants on a mountain. If this happens, the slope becomes bare, or empty. Without trees and other plants to hold the soil in place, landslides are much more likely. Steep hills are also more likely to have landslides.

A 2005 landslide destroyed these homes in Laguna Beach, California.

Landslides can be very destructive. Many people build their homes on hills and near the edges of cliffs. These buildings are in danger from a landslide. Every year landslides cause millions of dollars in damage to homes and property.

The problems caused by landslides can be lessened. The government can stop people from building in dangerous places. Support walls can be built that will push landslides away from homes and businesses. And before buying a home, people can ask experts if the site is likely to have landslides.

3. List three solutions that can help reduce problems caused by landslides.

Problem

Landslides can be destructive in places where people have built houses on hills and near the edges of cliffs.

Solution

a. Local governments can _____.

b. Landslides can be pushed away from homes by _____.

c. Before buying a home on a hill, people can _____.

Summary   A landslide is the sudden movement of loose rock and soil down a steep slope. Landslides cause rapid changes to Earth's surface. List three causes of landslides.

a. _____

b. _____

c. _____

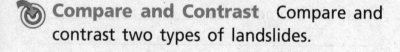 **Compare and Contrast**   Compare and contrast two types of landslides.

Mudslides		Rockslides
caused by _____ or sudden _____ of snow	sudden movement of loose rock and soil down a steep slope	caused by loosened _____ suddenly _____ from cliffs

Types of Landslides

There are many steep hills in mountain regions. Landslides happen a lot in these places. When the soil is wet, a large piece of it can slide down the hill. This type of landslide can carry away trees, cars, and houses.

Rockslides happen when loose rocks fall suddenly. Many rockslides happen on the steep cliffs in Yosemite Valley. They also happen in other places in California where there are steep, rocky hills.

LANDSLIDE
A mass of rocks and soil move downhill.

ROCKSLIDE
Large pieces of rock break off and fall down the hill.

COMPARE AND CONTRAST

Compare and contrast two types of landslides.

creep (kreep) Slow movement of land along a fault.

arrastre Movimiento lento de tierra a lo largo de una falla.

earthquake (URTH kwayk) A sudden movement of part of Earth's crust.

terremoto Movimiento repentino de la corteza terrestre.

epicenter (EHP ih sehn tur) Where an earthquake is felt most strongly or has its greatest intensity.

epicentro Lugar donde un terremoto se siente con más fuerza o intensidad.

fault (fawlt) A crack in Earth's crust.

falla Grieta en la corteza terrestre.

focus (FO kus) The point underground where an earthquake starts.

foco Punto bajo la superficie de la Tierra donde comienza un terremoto.

landslide (LAND slyd) The sudden movement of loose rock and soil down a steep slope.

deslizamiento de tierra Movimiento repentino de rocas sueltas y suelo en una pendiente.

Group two or more of the words on the page and explain why they go together.

Visit www.eduplace.com to play puzzles and word games.

(Circle) the words in this glossary that are the same in English and Spanish.

Glossary

lava (LAH vuh) Molten rock that reaches Earth's surface.

  lava Roca fundida que sale a la superficie de la Tierra.

magma (MAG muh) The molten rock beneath Earth's surface.

  magma Roca fundida que hay bajo la superficie de la Tierra.

seismology (syz MAHL uh jee) The study of earthquakes.

  sismología Estudio de los terremotos.

tsunami (tsoo NAH mee) A very large ocean wave caused by an earthquake that occurs on the ocean floor.

  maremoto Ola gigantesca de mar causada por un terremoto que tiene lugar en el suelo del océano.

volcano (vahl KAY noh) An opening in Earth's crust through which hot ash, gases, and molten rock escape from deep within Earth.

  volcán Apertura en la corteza terrestre por la que escapan cenizas calientes, gases y roca fundida del interior de la Tierra.

Responding

Think About What You Have Read

Vocabulary

❶ A crack in Earth's crust is called a/an _____.

A) tsunami

B) focus

C) epicenter

D) fault

Comprehension

❷ The study of earthquakes is called _____.

❸ A very large ocean wave that is caused by an underwater earthquake is a/an _____.

❹ Describe two kinds of movement that occur along faults.

Critical Thinking

❺ How might studying the causes of volcanoes help people?

Chapter Review

Vocabulary

❶ ⟨Circle⟩ the correct answer on the page.

Comprehension

❷ _____

❸ _____

❹ _____

_____

_____

Critical Thinking

❺ _____

_____

_____

Slow Changes on Earth

KWL

WHAT DO YOU KNOW?

List one fact or draw a picture to show something you know about each of these causes of slow changes on Earth:

a. Weathering _____

_____

_____

b. Erosion _____

_____

_____

c. How water shapes the land _____

_____

_____

d. How wind shapes the land _____

_____

_____

Contents

1 What Are Weathering and Erosion? 140

2 How Does Water Shape the Land? 144

3 How Do Ice and Wind Shape the Land? . . 148

Glossary 153

WHAT DO YOU WANT TO KNOW?

Skim the pictures and headings in this chapter. List one thing you want to find out about each of these causes of slow changes on Earth:

a. Weathering _____

_____

_____

b. Erosion _____

_____

_____

c. Water _____

_____

_____

d. Wind _____

_____

_____

Lesson Preview

VOCABULARY

erosion The movement of rock material from one place to another. *(noun)*

glacier A large mass of slow-moving ice. *(noun)*

weathering The slow wearing away of rock into smaller pieces. *(noun)*

VOCABULARY SKILL: Multiple-Meaning Words

The word *figure* is used in a caption in this lesson. This word has more than one meaning. Read the sentence. Write a meaning for *figure* other than the one used in the sentence.

Acid rain has damaged this stone *figure* on a building in Paris, France.

_____

_____

_____

5.a. Students know changes in the earth are caused by slow processes, such as erosion, and by rapid processes, such as landslides, volcanic eruptions, and earthquakes.

5.b. Students know natural processes, such as freezing and melting and growing plant roots, cause rocks to break into pieces.

5.c. Students know moving water wears away landforms; water reshapes the land by moving it from one place and depositing it in other places.

140

1 What Are Weathering and Erosion?

Earth's surface is built up and worn away slowly. Both processes change Earth's surface.

Weathering

Have you ever picked up a smooth stone at the beach? If you have, you have seen an example of weathering (WETH ur ihng). **Weathering** is the slow wearing away of rock into smaller pieces. Ice, plant roots, chemicals, and water can all cause weathering.

Most rocks have small cracks. In cold weather, water freezes in these cracks. The ice expands, or gets bigger. This makes the crack bigger, too. Over time, the freezing and melting causes rocks to break.

Weathering caused this huge boulder in Yosemite to break off from the top of the hill.

boulder

The roots of plants can break apart large rocks.

Acid rain has damaged this stone figure on a building in Paris, France.

Plant roots grow into the cracks. They also make the cracks expand. This breaks the rock.

Water flows over rocks and moves them. The rocks bump into each other again and again. As the rocks weather, sharp edges become smooth and the rocks get smaller.

When the outer layer of a rock gets very hot, it can peel off. Forest fires and the Sun can cause this. When cool rain falls on hot rocks, the rocks might break.

Chemicals can weather rocks. Chemicals are liquids and gases that cause something to change. Some gases mix with rainwater and turn it into acid rain. Acid rain weakens rock, causing it to break.

1. Weathering is the slow wearing away of rock into small pieces. List four causes of weathering.

   a. _____

   b. _____

   c. _____

   d. _____

2. Look at the picture of the stone figure. How did water and chemicals combine to weather the statue?

   _____

   _____

   _____

   _____

   _____

141

3. The moving of rock material from one place to another is called _____.

I Wonder . . . Which would erode more easily—rock that has been heavily weathered, or rock that has been weathered very little? What do you think?

_____

_____

_____

_____

_____

Erosion

After a big storm, have you seen soil and pebbles being carried by running water? If so, you have seen **erosion** (ih ROH zhuhn). Erosion is the moving of rock material from one place to another. What is caused by weathering is carried off by erosion.

Water is the main cause of erosion. Even a drop of water will loosen and pick up tiny particles of soil. As that water drop moves downhill, it will pick up more particles and carry them all away.

This balanced rock formation is the result of weathering and erosion.

Weathering and erosion happen over thousands and millions of years. Water from a river can break down rock. Over a very long time, that water will carry off enough weathered material to make a canyon. This is how the Grand Canyon was formed.

A **glacier** (GLAY shur) is a large piece of slow-moving ice. It moves so slowly that you cannot see it. As it moves, a glacier causes weathering and erosion of the rocks under it. A glacier can dig out huge areas of rock and soil to make valleys and canyons.

Wind is also a cause of weathering. Some places do not have plants to hold the soil down. In these places, the wind carries off dry sand and soil.

This U-shaped valley was shaped by moving water in the form of a glacier.

SEQUENCE

How do weathering and erosion form a deep canyon?

Summary   Earth's surface is slowly built up and worn down. The processes of weathering and erosion change Earth's surface. Complete the diagram to tell about weathering and erosion.

> The slow wearing away of rock into smaller pieces is called _____.

↓

> The materials that result from weathering are carried away by _____.

↓

> Three causes of erosion are _____, _____, and _____.

Sequence   How do weathering and erosion form a deep canyon?

_____

_____

_____

_____

VOCABULARY

bay A body of water that is partly enclosed by land and has a wide opening. *(noun)*

delta A large mass of sediment deposited at the mouth of a river. *(noun)*

deposition The dropping of sediment moved by water, wind, and ice. *(noun)*

headland A point of land, usually high, that extends out into the water. *(noun)*

river system The largest river and all the waterways that drain into it. *(noun)*

VOCABULARY SKILL: Root Words

The word *deposition* is based on the root word *deposit*, which means "to let fall." Read the definition of *deposition* above. Then use the meaning of *deposit* to write your own definition.

_____

_____

_____

5.a. Students know changes in the earth are caused by slow processes, such as erosion, and by rapid processes, such as landslides, volcanic eruptions, and earthquakes.

2 How Does Water Shape the Land?

Moving water changes Earth's surface. It does it through weathering, erosion, and deposition.

The Changing Coastline

Erosion moves bits of sand, soil, and rock. But what happens to that material?

Remember that bits of sand, soil, and rock are called sediment. The dropping of sediment moved by water, wind, and ice is called **deposition** (dehp uh ZIHSH uhn). Wind, glaciers, and moving water are the main causes of weathering, erosion, and deposition. At the beach, waves easily pick up and carry away sand. Waves also drop the sand, sometimes in new places.

Ocean waves can separate pieces of land to make tiny islands called sea stacks.

California's Coastline

California's beach coastline is made of eroded rock and shells. Ocean waves move sand along the shore.

Some beaches change with the season. In the winter, strong winds make strong waves. These waves remove more sand from the shore than they deposit. The beach becomes smaller. In summer, gentle waves leave more sand on the beach than they take. This makes the beach wider.

The California coastline also has headlands and bays. A **headland** is a high point of land that sticks out into the water. It has water on three sides. A **bay** is a body of water that is mostly surrounded by land. It has a wide opening called a mouth that connects the bay to the ocean.

Strong winter waves carry beach sand away and deposit it offshore.

Gentle summer waves deposit sand on the beach.

1. Complete the table to understand how some California beaches change with seasons.

Winter	Summer
• Strong _____ blow ocean water, producing strong _____.	• Gentle waves leave _____ sand on the beach than they _____.
• Strong waves remove _____ sand than they _____.	• The beach becomes _____.
• The beach becomes _____.	

2. a. A high point of land that extends into the water is called a _____.

   b. A body of water that is mostly surrounded by land is called a _____.

3. Complete the diagram to tell about river systems.

Streams join to form _____ .

↓

These flow into _____ .

↓

Together, they form a _____ .

4. List two river features formed by deposition.

a. _____

b. _____

What does a river deposit in a floodplain?

a. _____

b. _____

c. _____

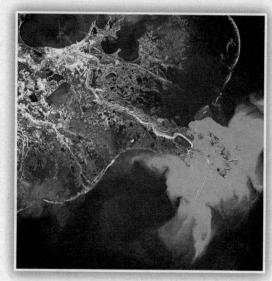

This alluvial fan is at the mouth of a glacial stream in Canada.

River Systems

Streams join to form a river. Small rivers join to make a large river. The biggest river and the water that flows into it are called a **river system**. Deposition makes many river system features.

Near its mouth, a river slows down. Then it drops sediment. This makes a delta. A **delta** is a large mass of sediment at the mouth of a river.

Deposition also makes an alluvial fan. This forms after a river runs down a steep hill. It looks like a fan.

Sometimes too much water flows down a river. The water has nowhere to go. It goes over the river's bank, or edge. This is a flood. The land where a river often floods is called a floodplain. Rivers deposit sand, silt, and clay in floodplains.

People Shape the Land

People also have an effect on the land. When they build dams on rivers, they change the regular flow of the water. This also keeps sediment from flowing down the river.

The Shasta Dam is in California's Central Valley. The dam controls the flood water of the Sacramento River. It also gives water to the farmers in the valley. These waters have helped make farming in this valley important. Central Valley now grows a quarter of all the food that Americans eat.

The Shasta Dam provides water for California's Central Valley.

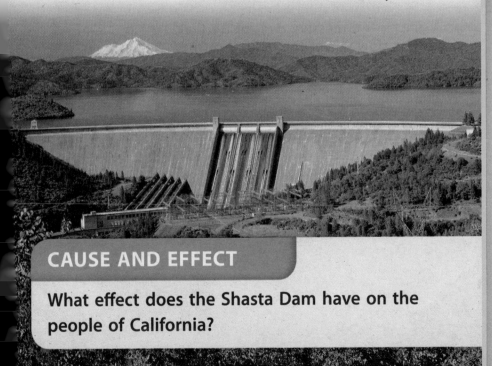

CAUSE AND EFFECT

What effect does the Shasta Dam have on the people of California?

Summary Moving water changes Earth's surface through weathering, erosion, and deposition. Complete the diagram to tell about features formed by deposition.

How does an alluvial fan form?

_____

_____

What is a delta?

_____

_____

How does a delta form?

_____

_____

What is a floodplain?

_____

_____

_____

🎯 **Cause and Effect** What effect does the Shasta Dam have on the people of California?

_____

_____

_____

147

VOCABULARY

erratic A single large boulder moved by a glacier and deposited when the glacier melts. *(noun)*

moraine The long ridge formed by boulders, rocks, and soil carried and deposited by a glacier. *(noun)*

sand dune A hill or pile of sand that was formed by the wind. *(noun)*

VOCABULARY SKILL: Word Origins

The word *erratic* can be traced back to the Latin word *errare* which means "to wander." Read the definition of *erratic* above. Explain how the Latin meaning of the word might relate to that definition.

_____

_____

_____

5.a. Students know changes in the earth are caused by slow processes, such as erosion, and by rapid processes, such as landslides, volcanic eruptions, and earthquakes.
5.c. Students know moving water wears away landforms; water reshapes the land by moving it from one place and depositing it in other places.

3 How Do Ice and Wind Shape the Land?

Glaciers and wind slowly wear down and build up the land.

Glaciers

A glacier flows down a hill. Glaciers formed long ago. They were made in cold places where snow piled up year after year. Finally, the pressure of the snow turned it into ice.

A glacier's weight makes it slow. As it moves, it erodes what is below it. Large amounts of soil and rock are pushed ahead. When glaciers melt, they change the land.

A glacier is a massive river of ice that pushes slowly over the land. It pushes rocks and soil ahead of it.

A glacier moved this land. Rain filled in where the land was to form June Lake in California.

What Glaciers Leave Behind

Glaciers leave signs of their changes. They change the land through erosion and deposition. They carry off tons of rock and soil. Then glaciers stop moving. They start to melt and deposit rocks and soil.

The long ridge, or raised piece of land, formed by the materials carried and deposited by a glacier is called a **moraine**. One large boulder deposited by a glacier when it melted is an **erratic**. A bowl-shaped hole left by a glacier is a cirque (surk).

1. Fill in the chart to tell about glaciers.

Year after year, _____ piles up.

↓

As more snow falls, _____ increases and turns the snow to _____.

↓

The weight of the ice makes the _____ move slowly. As it moves, it _____ the land.

2. List two signs of change left by glaciers through erosion and deposition.

a. _____

_____

b. _____

_____

3. Complete the diagram to summarize evidence of glaciers.

When rocks in glaciers scrape along Earth's surface, _____ form.

The long ridge formed by materials carried and deposited by a glacier is called a/an _____.

Evidence of Glaciers

A bowl-shaped hollow, or hole, left by a glacier is called a/an _____.

A large boulder deposited by a glacier when it melts is called a/an _____.

I Wonder . . . How might a glacier form a lake?

_____

_____

_____

_____

_____

_____

Evidence of Glaciers

Yosemite Valley in California was partly formed by glaciers. Glaciers left erratics, cirques, moraines, and grooves. They also made nearly all of the lakes.

Glaciers have helped make mountains and dig valleys. They have helped make some of the most beautiful landforms in the world.

Erratic

This large boulder dropped by a glacier is called an erratic.

Cirque

This bowl-shaped hollow is a cirque.

Moraine

This rock-strewn ridge is called a moraine.

Grooves

These grooves are made by rocks embedded in glaciers.

Wind Carves the Land

Wind is not as strong as water, but it can still change the shape of the land. Have you ever been to the beach on a windy day? Then you already know that the wind can carry sediment.

Wind easily picks up and carries sand. The stronger the wind, the more sand it will carry. Wind is more likely to cause erosion when it is dry. Dry sand is lighter and easier to carry.

Wind erosion is very strong when there are no plants. Windbreaks, or things that lessen the force of wind, such as fences, grass, and trees, can help stop wind erosion.

Sediment the wind carries also weather Earth's surface. Over time, they help shape rock formations like the one seen below.

This rock formation at the Grand Canyon was shaped by wind erosion.

Circle the word that makes each sentence true.

4. Wind easily picks up and carries (sand, ice).

   It is easier for wind to carry (dry, wet) sand.

5. Wind erosion is greatest where there are (few, many) plants.

6. List three windbreaks that lessen wind erosion.

   a. _____

   b. _____

   c. _____

I Wonder . . . Grass and trees help prevent landslides. Why might grass and trees also help lessen wind erosion?

_____

_____

_____

Summary   Glaciers are moving rivers of ice. Glaciers and wind slowly wear down and build up the land. Wind changes the land by picking up sediment in one place and depositing it in another. Look at the drawing below and complete the sentence.

This hill or pile of sand that was formed by wind is called a/an _____.

Compare and Contrast   How are a moraine and an erratic alike and different?

_____

_____

_____

Wind Builds Up the Land

Wind picks up sediment in one place and deposits it in another. The place where it is deposited is then built up.

Sand dunes form on seacoasts, in dry sandy places, and in deserts. A **sand dune** is a hill of sand that was made by the wind. Where there are strong winds, dunes can move as much as 30 km in a year. Dunes can bury towns, cities, and forests.

There are a lot of dunes along California's coast. The largest are the Monterey Bay dunes. California's coastal dunes were formed over thousands of years.

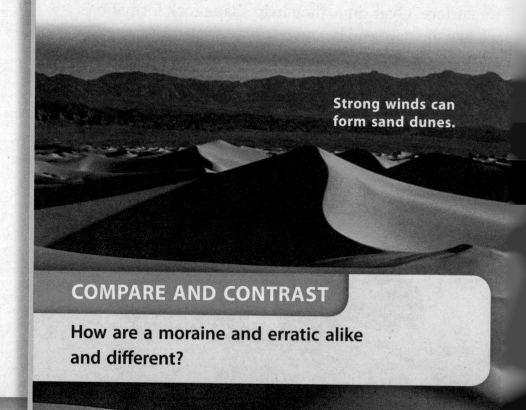

Strong winds can form sand dunes.

COMPARE AND CONTRAST

How are a moraine and erratic alike and different?

bay (bay) A body of water that is partly enclosed by land and has a wide opening.

> **bahía** Masa de agua limitada por tierra y con una gran entrada al mar.

delta (DEHL tah) A large mass of sediment deposited at the mouth of a river.

> **delta** Gran masa de sedimentos depositados en la boca de un río.

deposition (dehp uh ZIHSH uhn) The dropping of sediment moved by water, wind, and ice.

> **sedimentación** Caída de sedimento arrastrado por el agua, el viento o el hielo.

erosion (ih ROH zhuhn) The movement of rock material from one place to another.

> **erosión** Desplazamiento de material de roca de un lugar a otro.

erratic (ih RAH tihk) A single large boulder moved by a glacier and deposited when the glacier melts.

> **roca errática** Gran canto rodado movido por un glaciar y depositado en el lugar donde el glaciar se descongela.

glacier (GLAY shur) A large mass of slow-moving ice.

> **glaciar** Gran masa de hielo que se mueve lentamente.

Group two or more of the words on the page and explain why they go together.

Circle the English words and their meanings for all the glossary words that relate to glaciers.

Glossary

headland (HED land) A point of land, usually high, that extends out into the water.

cabo Punta de tierra, generalmente elevada, que se extiende hacia el mar.

moraine (MOH rayn) The long ridge formed by boulders, rocks, and soil carried and deposited by a glacier.

morrena Estructura alargada formada por cantos rodados, rocas y suelo transportados y depositados por un glaciar.

river system (RIH vur sys tehm) The largest river and all the waterways that drain into it.

sistema fluvial Un río grande y todos sus afluentes.

sand dune (sand DOON) A hill or pile of sand that was formed by the wind.

duna de arena Colina de arena formada por el viento.

weathering (WETH ur ihng) The slow wearing away of rock into smaller pieces.

desgaste Erosión lenta de la roca al deshacerse en trozos más pequeños.

Think About What You Have Read

Vocabulary

❶ A hill of sand that was formed by the wind is a/an _____.

    A) sand dune

    B) headland

    C) erratic

    D) delta

Comprehension

❷ A large mass of slow-moving ice is called a/an _____.

❸ What area of California was formed by glaciers?

❹ What happens when a river or a stream slows down?

Critical Thinking

❺ What would you predict would happen to the coastline if a glacier melted next to it? Explain.

WHAT DID YOU LEARN?

Vocabulary

❶ Circle the correct answer on the page.

Comprehension

❷ _____

    _____

❸ _____

    _____

❹ _____

    _____

Critical Thinking

❺ _____

    _____

    _____

WHAT DO YOU KNOW?

For each topic listed below write one fact or draw a picture to show something you know about electricity.

a. How electric charges behave

_____

_____

b. What an electric current is

_____

_____

c. How electricity is used

_____

_____

Electricity

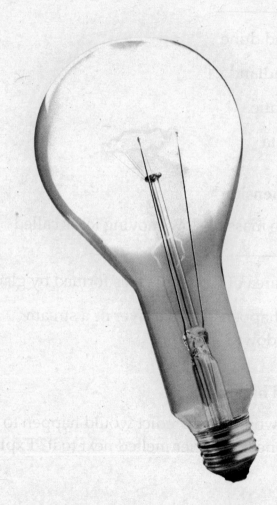

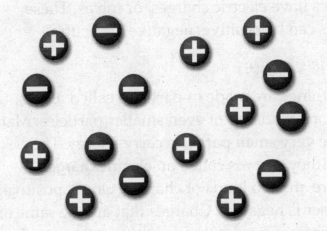

Contents

1 How Do Charges Behave?............. 158

2 What Is Electric Current?............. 161

3 How Is Electricity Used? 168

Glossary................................ 172

WHAT DO YOU WANT TO KNOW?

Skim the pictures and headings in this chapter. List one thing you want to find out about each of these topics.

a. The behavior of charges and electric current

_____

_____

_____

b. Circuits and switches

_____

_____

_____

c. The uses of electricity

_____

_____

_____

What else do you want to know about electricity?

_____

_____

_____

VOCABULARY

electric charges Units of electricity. *(noun)*

static electricity A built-up electric charge. *(noun)*

VOCABULARY SKILL: Antonyms

Antonyms are words with opposite meanings. For example, the word *tall* is an antonym of the word *short*. Give examples of an antonym for these words used in your text:

attract: _____

negative: _____

like: _____

1.e. Students know objects that have an electric charge attract or repel each other.

1 How Do Charges Behave?

All objects are made of small particles. Some particles have electric charges, or forces. These charges can be positive, negative, or neutral.

Electric Charges

All things are made of particles called atoms. Atoms are made up of even smaller particles. Many of these very small particles carry energy. The energy they carry is called an **electric charge**.

There are two kinds of charges. One is positive. The other is negative. Charges that are the same are like charges. Charges that are different are unlike charges. Some things have the same number of positive and negative charges. They are neutral. Most things are neutral.

electrically neutral	negatively charged	positively charged
an object that has the same number of positive and negative charges	an object that has more negative than positive charges	an object that has more positive than negative charges

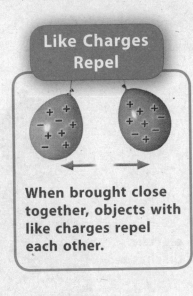

Like Charges Repel

When brought close together, objects with like charges repel each other.

Unlike Charges Attract

When brought close together, objects with unlike charges attract each other.

How Charges Behave

Electric charges affect each other. Like charges repel, or push each other away. Unlike charges attract, or pull toward one another. So two positive charges push each other away. But a negative charge and a positive charge pull toward each other.

Negative charges move easily from object to object. Positive charges do not.

Negative charges usually are not attracted to neutral charges. But you can make negative charges move. Rubbing can move them from one object to another. For example, when you rub a balloon with a wool cloth, it makes the negative charges move from the cloth to the balloon.

1. Look at the charged particles shown in the boxes below. Tell how the charges will behave toward each other by labeling each box *attract* or *repel.*

2. Which type of charge moves easily? Circle the correct term. (positive negative)

Summary All objects are made up of tiny particles. Many of these tiny particles carry positive or negative electric charges. An object can be electrically neutral or it can have a total negative charge or a positive charge.

What happens when you touch an object that has a built-up electric charge?

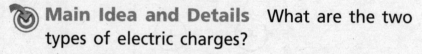

Main Idea and Details What are the two types of electric charges?

Label the art below to describe the two types of electric charges.

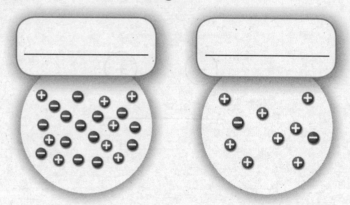

Buildup and Discharge

Sometimes a charge builds up. This built-up electric charge is called **static electricity** (STAT ihk ih lehk TRIHS ih tee).

You can get a shock when you touch a metal doorknob. This shock is a form of electric discharge. A negative charge has built up on the boy in the picture. When he touches the doorknob, the charge jumps from him to the knob. The release of a built-up negative charge is called an electric discharge, or spark.

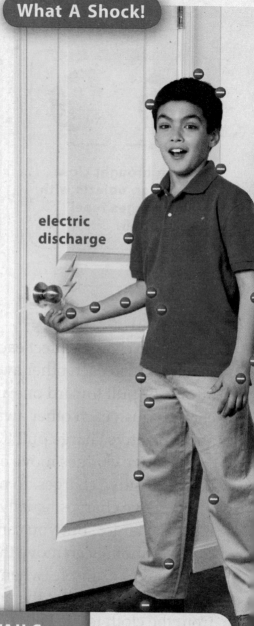

electric discharge

MAIN IDEA AND DETAILS

What are the two types of electric charges?

160

2 What Is Electric Current?

An electric circuit is a path that charges follow. Electric circuits can be used to change electrical energy into other kinds of energy.

How Charges Move

You wake up to an alarm clock. You turn on your light. Later, you toast bread. You converted, or changed, the energy of charged particles. You changed them to sound, light, and heat.

You learned about static electricity. Those charges either stay in place or suddenly discharge. That energy is not useful.

You want the energy of charged particles to be useful. To do so, you must control it. What if energy were always flowing through something? Then it could not be simply building up. That energy would be controlled and used. The continuous flow of electric charges is called an **electric current**.

VOCABULARY

battery A device that converts chemical energy to electrical energy. *(noun)*

conductor A material through which charged particles flow easily. *(noun)*

electric circuit The pathway that electric current follows. *(noun)*

electric current Continuous flow of electric charges. *(noun)*

insulator A material that electric charges do not flow through easily. *(noun)*

parallel circuit A circuit in which the parts are connected so that electric current passes along more than one pathway. *(noun)*

series circuit A circuit in which the parts are connected so that electric current passes through each part, one after another, along a single pathway. *(noun)*

1.a. Students know how to build simple series circuits and parallel circuits using wires, batteries, and bulbs.
1.g. Students know electrical energy can be changed to heat, light, and motion.

1. What is an electric current?

_____

2. Compare and contrast conductors and insulators.

Conductors	Insulators
Charges _____ easily.	Charges _____ easily.
List three examples: _____ _____ _____	List three examples: _____ _____ _____

I Wonder . . . Plastic is a good insulator. Can electric charges pass through a plastic bottle that is full of water and has a plastic cap?

_____

_____

_____

_____

162

Conductors and Insulators

Electric current easily passes through metals like copper, aluminum, gold, and silver. These metals are good conductors. A **conductor** (kuhn DUHK tuhr) is something that negatively charged particles flow through easily.

Charges flow easily through tap water. Tap water has particles that make it a good conductor. Because the cells of all living things have water, they are conductors, too.

Charges have a hard time flowing through some things. They are called **insulators** (IHN suh lay tuhrz). Wood, air, and glass are insulators.

Together, conductors and insulators control the flow of electric charges.

How a Toaster Works

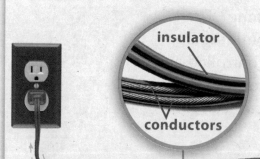

insulator

conductors

2 Charges move through the heating coils, causing them to become hot.

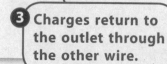

1 When the toaster is turned on, electric charges flow from the outlet, through one copper wire, to heating coils in the toaster.

3 Charges return to the outlet through the other wire.

Circuits and Switches

The path that an electric current follows is an **electric circuit** (ih lehk trihk SUR kiht). A circuit is closed if it does not have any gaps or openings. Electric charges can flow through it.

If there is a gap in the circuit, you have an open circuit. When a circuit is open, electric charges cannot flow through it.

Most circuits have a switch. A switch opens and closes the circuit. A switch lets you turn a light bulb on, closing the circuit. It also lets you turn the light bulb off, opening the circuit. Pushing a doorbell also closes a circuit, causing the bell to ring.

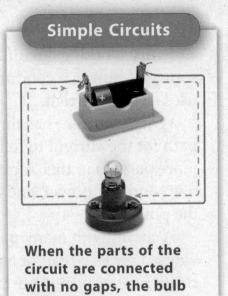

Simple Circuits

When the parts of the circuit are connected with no gaps, the bulb will light.

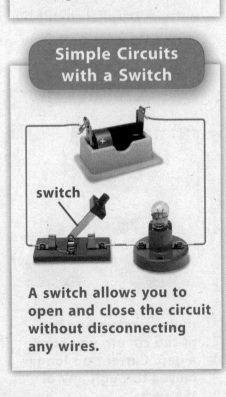

Simple Circuits with a Switch

switch

A switch allows you to open and close the circuit without disconnecting any wires.

3. Complete the diagram to tell about circuits and switches.

In an electric circuit, electric current follows a/an _____.

↓

An open circuit is one that has a/an _____, and electric charges _____ flow through it.

↓

Most circuits include a switch that _____ and _____ the circuit.

163

4. What three parts does every working circuit have?

a. _____

b. _____

c. _____

Correctly complete each sentence to tell about circuits.

5. Current passes through each part of the circuit along a single pathway in a/an

_____ circuit.

6. Current passes along more than one pathway

in a/an _____ circuit.

7. How is a parallel circuit different from a series circuit?

_____

_____

_____

Two Types of Circuits

Every working circuit has at least three parts: a source of power, a conductor, and something that uses electric current.

When a current has three parts, there is only one path for the current to follow. But a current can have more parts than this. It can have a switch, more than one source of power, and more than one user of the power.

A circuit with many parts can be made in two ways: a series circuit or a parallel circuit. A **series circuit** has connected parts. The electric current passes through each part, one by one, along a single path. A **parallel circuit** has its parts connected so the current passes along more than one pathway.

Series Circuits	Parallel Circuits

If you remove one part of the circuit, you create a gap. Current no longer moves through any of the parts.	If you remove one part from the circuit, current can still move through the other parts.

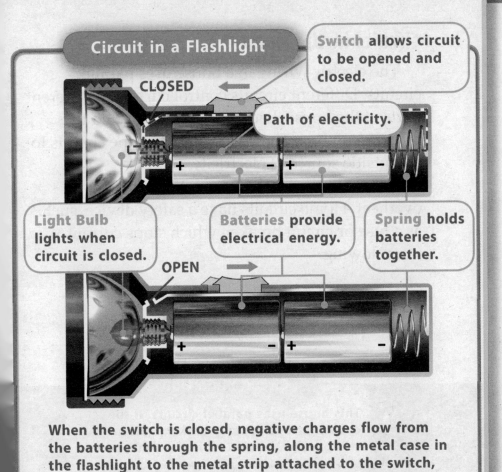

Circuit in a Flashlight

Switch allows circuit to be opened and closed.

CLOSED

Path of electricity.

Light Bulb lights when circuit is closed.

OPEN

Batteries provide electrical energy.

Spring holds batteries together.

When the switch is closed, negative charges flow from the batteries through the spring, along the metal case in the flashlight to the metal strip attached to the switch, to the bulb holder, through the light bulb, and back to the batteries.

Circuits Without Wires

Circuits can use any conductor. Current will flow as long as the conductor is connected to a constant source of electricity.

One source of electrical energy is a battery. A **battery** changes chemical energy into electrical energy. In a flashlight, the batteries form part of the circuit.

8. Use your finger to trace the flow of electric current through the flashlight.

   a. What is the source of electrical energy?

   _____

   b. What does this source do?

   _____

I Wonder . . . Does a flashlight use a series circuit or a parallel circuit? What do you think?

_____

_____

_____

_____

165

9. Which type of circuit is used for electrical wiring in a house?

_____

I Wonder . . . Look at the picture of the circuits in a house. The lights and appliances in the kitchen are receiving no electricity. The lights in the living room are all working. How is this possible?

_____

_____

_____

_____

Circuits in the Home

The electric wiring in a house uses parallel circuits. Different circuits control current in different parts of the house. Each circuit is connected to a main circuit box. The box connects all the circuits to an outside source of electricity.

If there is too much current, the wires can overheat. Home circuits have a safety device, such as a fuse or circuit breaker, which stops current from flowing.

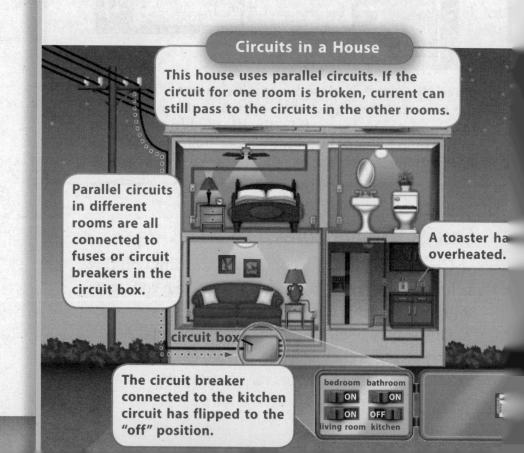

Circuits in a House

This house uses parallel circuits. If the circuit for one room is broken, current can still pass to the circuits in the other rooms.

Parallel circuits in different rooms are all connected to fuses or circuit breakers in the circuit box.

A toaster ha overheated.

circuit box

The circuit breaker connected to the kitchen circuit has flipped to the "off" position.

bedroom	bathroom
ON	ON
ON	OFF
living room	kitchen

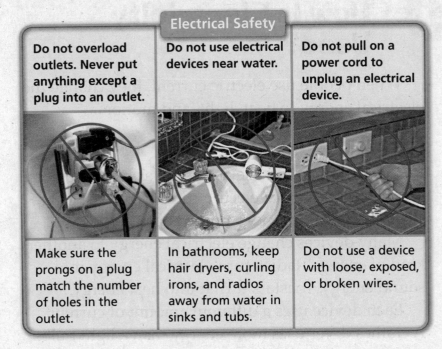

Electrical Safety		
Do not overload outlets. Never put anything except a plug into an outlet.	Do not use electrical devices near water.	Do not pull on a power cord to unplug an electrical device.
Make sure the prongs on a plug match the number of holes in the outlet.	In bathrooms, keep hair dryers, curling irons, and radios away from water in sinks and tubs.	Do not use a device with loose, exposed, or broken wires.

Electrical Safety

The human body uses electrical energy. Electrical signals make the heart beat and carry information from the brain to other parts of the body.

Never touch exposed electric wires. Never put a conductor, like metal, near an electric current. This could cause electric current to pass through your body. Electric current is dangerous in other ways, too. See the chart above for tips on how to stay safe around electricity.

COMPARE AND CONTRAST

How is electric current different from static electricity?

Summary   An electric circuit is a pathway that an electric current follows. Electric circuits can be used to change electrical energy into other forms of energy.

List three ways to stay safe around electricity.

a. _____

_____

b. _____

_____

c. _____

_____

Compare and Contrast   Complete the diagram to compare electric current and static electricity.

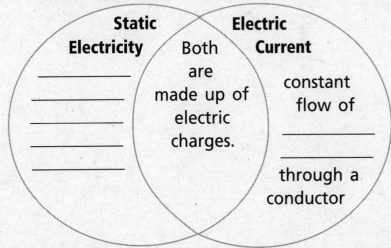

Static Electricity

Electric Current

Both are made up of electric charges.

constant flow of

through a conductor

167

VOCABULARY

resistance The ability of a material to slow down or stop electric current. *(noun)*

watt A unit of measure of electrical power. *(noun)*

VOCABULARY SKILL: Suffixes

The word *resistance* has the suffix *-ance,* which means "the act of." Based on your knowledge of the word *resist,* use the meaning of *-ance* to write your own definition for the word *resistance.*

  1.g. Students know electrical energy can be changed to heat, light, and motion.

3 How Is Electricity Used?

When people use electric current, they change the electrical energy to heat, light, and motion.

Electricity in Homes

Clocks, lights, and televisions are electrical devices. They get energy from electric current. You use electric current dozens of times a day.

Many devices change electrical energy to another kind of energy. Radios turn electrical energy into sound energy. Toasters turn it into heat energy.

Each device uses a different amount of current. A clothes dryer uses more energy than a light bulb. A **watt** is a unit of measure of electrical power.

A television changes electrical energy to light energy and sound energy.

The car gets electrical energy from batteries. The electrical energy is changed to motion.

Converting Electricity to Heat

Some devices, such as toasters, ovens, and hair dryers, convert electrical energy to heat.

How do these items work? In a hair dryer, the current flows through a conductor to the heating unit. The cord is the conductor. The heating unit has a resistance to the current. **Resistance** is the ability to slow down or stop the flow of electric current.

When the current meets resistance, the heating unit gets hot. The heat made can be used to dry hair. It could also be used to cook food or warm a house.

Heating units can get very hot. They can stay hot, too. Sometimes they stay hot for several minutes after the current has been turned off.

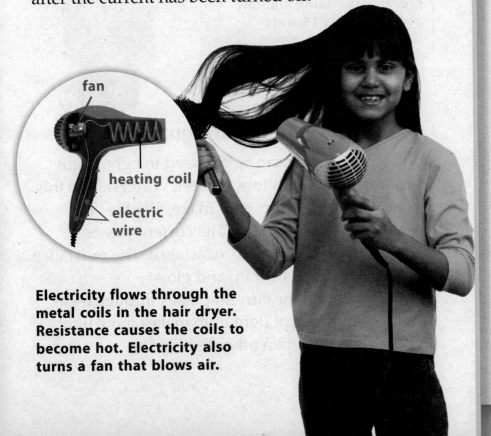

fan

heating coil

electric wire

Electricity flows through the metal coils in the hair dryer. Resistance causes the coils to become hot. Electricity also turns a fan that blows air.

1. List three kinds of energy to which electrical energy can be changed.

   a. _____

   b. _____

   c. _____

2. How is electricity measured?

   _____

3. Complete the sentences to tell how a hair dryer works.

   a. Electricity flows through _____ in the hair dryer.

   b. They become hot when the current meets _____.

   c. Electricity also turns a/an _____ that blows hot air that dries the hair.

169

4. List two devices that change electrical energy into light.

a. _____

b. _____

5. What role does resistance play in changing electric current into light?

_____

_____

_____

6. For each pair, (circle) the device that saves more energy.

regular light bulb

fluorescent light bulb

regular TV screen

flat-panel TV screen

COMPUTER MONITOR
Computer monitors and television screens change electrical energy to light energy. Flat-panel screens are more energy-efficient than regular screens.

ENERGY-SAVING BULB
Regular bulbs use 40 to 60 watts of electricity to produce the same amount of light that a 15-watt fluorescent lamp produces.

Converting Electricity to Light

Electrical energy can be changed to light. Light bulbs, computer monitors, and televisions all do this.

The way electrical energy makes light is very close to how it makes heat. The current passes through a material that has resistance. The resistance makes the material heat up and glow.

In a light bulb, the current passes through a gas or wire. A fluorescent light bulb makes more light and uses less heat than other light bulbs.

Converting Electricity to Motion

Some devices change electricity to motion. Motion is movement. Motion is useful for many kinds of work.

The motor in a power tool makes motion from electrical energy. In a drill, the motor turns a drill bit. In a saw, the motor turns a sharp blade.

Wheelchairs and scooters use electrical energy. So do some cars. A hybrid is a car that uses gas and an electric motor. The car needs less gas because of the electric motor. This is good for the environment.

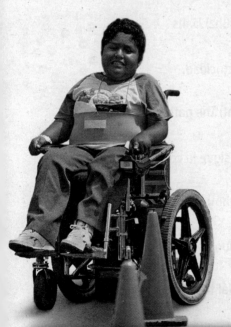

Power tools convert electricity to motion.

A large battery provides electricity for this wheelchair.

MAIN IDEA AND DETAILS

How does a light bulb use resistance to produce light?

Summary When people use electric current, they change the electrical energy to heat, sound, light, and the energy of motion.

Complete the table to give an example of an appliance that changes electrical energy in each way.

What Electricity Is Changed To . . .	Example
Sound	
Heat	
Light	
Motion	

Main Idea and Details How does a light bulb use resistance to produce light?

_____

_____

_____

Write a single sentence using as many words from the page as you can.

_____

_____

_____

_____

battery (ba tur REE) A device that converts chemical energy to electrical energy.

batería Dispositivo que convierte la energía química en energía eléctrica.

conductor (kuhn DUHK tuhr) A material through which charged particles flow easily.

conductor Material a través del cual circulan fácilmente las partículas con carga.

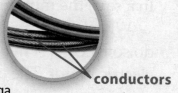
conductors

electric charges (EE lehk trihk charjuhz) Units of electricity.

carga eléctrica Unidades de electricidad.

electric circuit (ih lehk trihk SUR kiht) The pathway that electric current follows.

circuito eléctrico Recorrido que sigue la corriente eléctrica.

electric current (ih lehk trihk KUR uhnt) Continuous flow of electric charges.

corriente eléctrica Fluido continuo de cargas eléctricas.

insulator (IHN suh lay tuhr) A material that electric charges do not flow through easily.

aislante Material a través del cual las partículas eléctricas no circulan fácilmente.

insulator

Glossary

parallel circuit (PAYR eh lehl SUHR kiht) A circuit in which the parts are connected so that electric current passes along more than one pathway.

circuito paralelo Circuito cuyas partes están conectadas de modo tal que la corriente eléctrica hace más de un recorrido.

resistance (ree ZIH stans) The ability of a material to slow down or stop electric current.

resistencia Capacidad de un material para desacelerar o detener la corriente eléctrica.

series circuit (seer EEZ SUHR kiht) A circuit in which the parts are connected so that electric current passes through each part, one after another, along a single pathway.

circuito en serie Circuito en el que las partes están conectadas de modo que la corriente eléctrica pasa por cada parte, una tras otra, a lo largo de un solo recorrido.

static electricity (STAT ihk ih lehk TRIHS ih tee) A built-up electric charge.

electricidad estática Carga eléctrica contenida.

watt (waht) A unit of measure of electrical power.

vatio Unidad que mide la energía eléctrica.

Visit www.eduplace.com to play puzzles and word games.

Circle the English words and their meanings for all the glossary words.

Chapter Review

WHAT DID YOU LEARN?

Vocabulary

❶ (Circle) the correct answer on the page.

Comprehension

❷ _____

❸ _____

❹ _____

_____

Critical Thinking

❺ _____

_____

_____

_____

174

Think About What You Have Read

Vocabulary

❶ A complete path that an electric current can travel on is a/an _____.

A) watt

B) electric current

C) electric circuit

D) parallel circuit

Comprehension

❷ A device that converts chemical energy into electrical energy is a/an _____.

❸ Two objects attract each other if they have opposite _____.

❹ What forms of energy can electric current be converted into?

Critical Thinking

❺ You reach for a doorknob and receive a small shock. Use what you know about static electricity to explain this.

WHAT DO YOU KNOW?

List one fact about each of these topics.

a. How magnets behave _____

_____

_____

b. Earth's magnetic field _____

_____

_____

c. How electromagnets are used _____

_____

_____

d. How energy can be saved _____

_____

_____

Magnetism and Electromagnets

Contents

1 How Do Magnets Behave? 178

2 What Is Earth's Magnetic Field? 181

3 How Are Electromagnets Used? 184

4 How Can Energy Be Conserved? 189

Glossary 192

WHAT DO YOU WANT TO KNOW?

Skim the pictures and headings in this chapter. List one thing you want to find out about each of these topics.

a. How magnets behave _____

_____

_____

b. Earth's magnetic field _____

_____

_____

c. How electromagnets are used _____

_____

_____

d. How energy can be saved _____

_____

_____

1

How Do Magnets Behave?

VOCABULARY

magnet An object that attracts certain metals. *(noun)*

magnetic field The space in which the force of a magnet can act. *(noun)*

magnetic poles Two areas where the force of a magnet is at its greatest. *(noun)*

permanent magnet An object that keeps its magnetism for a long time. *(noun)*

temporary magnet An object that loses its magnetism after a short time. *(noun)*

VOCABULARY SKILL: Word Parts

The word *magnetic* has the suffix *-ic*, which means "associated with or dealing with." Use this information and your knowledge of magnets to write your own definition for the word *magnetic*.

_____

_____

Magnets are objects that pull, or attract, certain metals. They have magnetic poles and magnetic fields where the force acts.

Properties of Magnets

A **magnet** (MAG niht) is an object that attracts certain metals. It is most attracted to iron. Magnets do not attract all metal. They also do not attract wood, plastic, or rubber.

A magnet's power gets weaker the farther away it is. If you hold a magnet next to a refrigerator (whose door is made of iron), the magnet will be strongly attracted. But if you pull the magnet away, the force will get weaker.

If the particles making up an object line up, the object is a magnet.

bar magnet

eraser

1.f. Students know that magnets have a north pole and a south pole; they know that poles that are alike repel each other and poles that are different attract each other.

horseshoe magnet

bar magnet

ring magnets

A **permanent magnet** keeps its magnetism for a long time. A **temporary magnet** loses its magnetism quickly. You can make a temporary magnet by rubbing a metal, like a nail, against a permanent magnet.

The force of a magnet is greatest at its **magnetic poles**. On a horseshoe magnet and bar magnet, the poles are at the ends. On a ring magnet, the poles are on the top and bottom faces.

You know that unlike charges attract. They pull toward each other. Magnets act the same. Unlike poles of magnets attract each other. Like poles repel.

1. Complete the sentences in the diagram to tell about properties of magnets.

An object that attracts certain metals is called a _____.

A magnet that keeps its magnetism for a long time is a _____ _____.

A magnet's force is greatest at its _____ _____.

Stroking an iron object with a permanent magnet can make the object into a _____ _____.

2. (Circle) the word that makes each sentence true.

   a. Unlike poles of magnets (attract, repel) each other.

   b. Like poles of magnets (attract, repel) each other.

Summary Magnets are objects that attract certain metals, such as iron. Magnets have magnetic poles where the force of a magnet is greatest. Magnets also have magnetic fields, the space where the magnet's force can act. Fill in the table to tell about magnetic fields.

Observation	Explanation
You hold a magnet far away from a refrigerator door. The magnet and the steel door are not attracted.	The magnetic field gets _____ the farther you move away from the magnet.
You shake iron filings over a bar magnet. More filings group near the ends of the magnet.	The magnetic field is strongest near a magnet's _____.

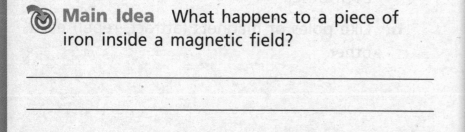

Main Idea What happens to a piece of iron inside a magnetic field?

_____

_____

_____

180

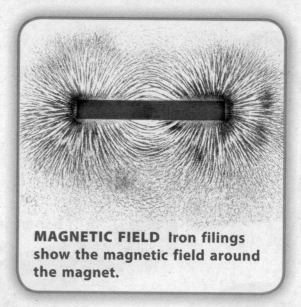

MAGNETIC FIELD Iron filings show the magnetic field around the magnet.

Magnetic Fields

The space where a magnet's force can act is its **magnetic field** (MAG neh tik feeld). Look at the picture above. You can see the magnetic field. It is made by the iron filings around the magnet. There are more iron filings near the poles. That is where the pull is strongest.

A magnet will attract any iron object in its magnetic field. But the magnet will not act on anything outside the field. Magnetic force can act through air and water. It acts through some other objects, too.

MAIN IDEA

What happens to a piece of iron inside a magnetic field?

What Is Earth's Magnetic Field?

2

Earth acts like a giant magnet. It has a magnetic field and magnetic poles. This is why compasses work. It also causes many effects on and around Earth.

Earth's Magnetic Field

Earth acts like a magnet. It has iron at its center. As Earth spins, the iron lines up. This makes our magnetic field. Like a magnet, Earth has two poles.

A compass works because Earth has a magnetic field.

Lesson Preview

VOCABULARY

aurora A display of lights in the sky caused by particles from the Sun interacting with Earth's magnetic field and atmosphere. *(noun)*

compass An instrument that senses magnetic north using a free-moving magnet. *(noun)*

VOCABULARY SKILL: Word Origins

The word *aurora* comes from the word *aus-*, which means "to shine." Read the definition of *aurora*. Tell how the idea of shining is related to *aurora*.

_____

_____

1.b. Students know how to build a simple compass and can use it to show Earth's magnetic field.

181

1. To which direction does a compass needle point?

_____

a. (Circle) the photo of the compass. In which direction is the needle pointing?

_____

b. What type of magnet is a compass's needle?

_____

2. How does a compass interact with Earth?

_____

_____

_____

How a Compass Works

Before people knew Earth had a magnetic field, they used compasses. A **compass** is a tool that helps us find north.

The needle of a compass is a permanent magnet. It turns freely. The needle turns until it points toward the north pole.

EARTH'S MAGNETIC FIELD Earth acts like a giant magnet. The north-seeking pole of a compass needle is attracted to Earth's magnetic north pole.

Auroras are most often visible near Earth's north and south magnetic poles.

Auroras

Near the north and south poles, there are sometimes beautiful lights in the night sky. These are called **auroras** (uh ROHR uhz). An aurora is caused by particles from the Sun mixing with Earth's magnetic field.

The Sun sends out waves of small particles. This is called the solar wind. Earth's magnetic field catches some of these particles. They are pulled toward our poles. When the particles collide with Earth's atmosphere, they start to glow. We see it as lights in the sky.

CAUSE AND EFFECT

What causes auroras?

Summary   Earth acts like a giant magnet, with a magnetic field and magnetic poles. This property of Earth allows compasses to work and causes many effects on and around Earth. Look at the diagram. Then complete the sentences to tell how Earth acts like a magnet.

a. Earth's center is made up mostly of

_____.

b. The particles that make up the iron in Earth's center line up as Earth

_____.

c. This lining up of particles gives Earth a(n)

_____.

d. Like a magnet, Earth also has two

_____.

Cause and Effect   What causes auroras?

Cause	Effect
_____ _____ _____	auroras

VOCABULARY

electromagnet A strong temporary magnet that uses electricity to produce magnetism. *(noun)*

generator A device that uses magnetism to convert energy of motion into electrical energy. *(noun)*

motor A device that changes electrical energy to energy of motion. *(noun)*

VOCABULARY SKILL: Prefixes

The word *electromagnet* has the prefix *electro-*, which means "electric." Read the definition of *electromagnet* above. Based on your knowledge of the word *magnet*, use the meaning of *electro-* to write your own definition for the word *electromagnet*.

_____

_____

---

3 How Are Electromagnets Used?

Electricity can cause magnetism. Magnetism can make electricity.

Using Electromagnets

When you use electricity, you are using electromagnets (ih lehk troh MAG nihts). An **electromagnet** is a strong temporary magnet that uses electricity. You can make a weak temporary magnet by rubbing iron against a permanent magnet. You can make a strong temporary magnet by using electricity to make the magnetism.

When electric current goes through a wire, the current makes a weak magnetic field. If the wire is wrapped around iron, the magnetic field is stronger. Then the iron becomes magnetized. That is how electricity causes magnetism.

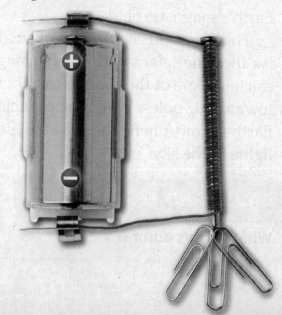

The nail acts as an electromagnet when the circuit is closed and the electric current flows through the wire.

Electromagnets act like other magnets. They attract things made of iron. They are surrounded by magnetic fields.

But the magnetic force of an electromagnet can be controlled. Increasing the amount of wire around the magnet makes the force stronger. Increasing the current running through the wire strengthens the force.

An electromagnet can be turned on and off. As soon as you stop sending an electric current through the wire, the electromagnet loses its pull.

Electromagnets are very useful. Cranes with strong electromagnets can pick up cars. But smaller electromagnets are used every day in the home. They are inside things like blenders, disk drives, and doorbells.

1 The electromagnet attracts scrap metal and moves it.

2 When the current is turned off, the crane is no longer magnetized and the metal drops into the pile.

1. How are electromagnets like other magnets?

_____

_____

2. List three ways the force of an electromagnet can be controlled.

a. _____

_____

b. _____

_____

c. _____

_____

3. An electric motor is a device that changes

_____ energy into _____.

4. Complete the diagram to tell how an electric motor works.

| When a motor is turned on, _____ passes through a wire that is wrapped around _____. |

↓

| A/an _____ is formed around both magnets in a motor. |

↓

| Motion is made when these magnetic fields _____ and _____ each other. |

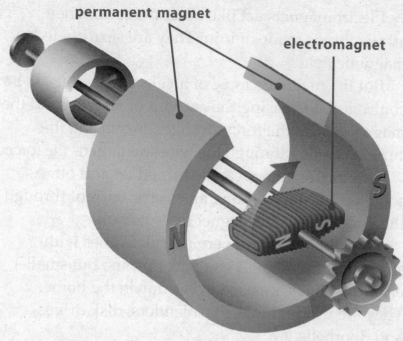

permanent magnet

electromagnet

N   S

This is a motor. Magnets help a motor run.

Motors

Refrigerators, mixers, and ceiling fans all have an electric motor. A **motor** is a device that changes electrical energy to energy of motion.

All motors have electromagnets and permanent magnets. When a motor is turned on, electric current passes through a wire wrapped around iron. This creates a magnetic field around both magnets. These magnetic fields then push and pull on each other, and motion is made.

Generating Electricity

You now know that a motor changes electrical energy into energy of motion. A generator does the opposite. A **generator** (JEHN uh ray tuhr) is a device that uses magnetism to change motion energy into electrical energy.

Giant generators produce electricity for cities. These generators have powerful permanent magnets.

There are two ways to increase the electricity made by a generator. You can use stronger permanent magnets or increase the amount of wire that wraps around the magnets.

The motion energy that a generator uses can come from falling water, wind, or a nuclear power plant.

ENERGY SOURCE Energy from falling water or burning fuels turns generator coils, producing electricity.

ELECTRIC POWER LINES Power lines carry electricity to customers.

HOMES AND BUSINESSES Although generated far away, electricity is as close as the nearest light switch.

5. Complete the diagram about generators.

Cause	Effect
The number of coils of wire in a generator is increased.	The amount of _____ produced by the generator is _____.
Energy from burning _____ turns generator _____.	Electricity is produced.

Summary Electricity can produce magnetism, and magnetism can produce electricity. Complete the diagram about the cost of electricity.

Some devices, like fans and toasters, use _____ only part of the time.

Refrigerators and _____ run 24 hours a day.

Cost of Electricity

Electricity is lost when devices _____ it as _____.

🎯 **Compare and Contrast** How are electric motors and generators different?

_____

_____

_____

188

The Cost of Using Electricity

Using electricity costs money. The cost of using an electric device depends on how much energy it takes to run and how long you run it. Some things, like fans and toasters, use electricity only part of the time. Others, like refrigerators and clocks, use electricity 24 hours a day.

Not all the electricity that people pay for is used to run devices. Some electricity is lost as it passes from conductor to conductor. Other electricity is lost when devices waste it as heat.

Appliances are now being built to use electricity without wasting as much. These appliances cost less to use.

Computers need electricity to run.

COMPARE AND CONTRAST

How are electric motors and generators different?

How Can Energy Be Conserved?

Electricity uses natural resources, so saving electricity helps save resources. Finding other sources of electrical energy can also lessen pollution.

Reasons to Conserve

Power plants use generators. Generators need energy. Most plants burn fossil fuels to get that energy. Coal, oil, and natural gas are **fossil fuels**.

The supply of fossil fuels on Earth is limited. That means we will run out of them. Burning fossil fuels also makes pollution. It adds smoke and gases to the air.

Smog, the mixture of smoke and fog, is a kind of air pollution. Many cities have smog from burning fossil fuels.

VOCABULARY

fossil fuels Natural fuels such as coal, oil, or natural gas. (*noun phrase*)

VOCABULARY SKILL: Word Derivation

Sometimes you can figure out the meaning of an unfamiliar term by finding out what each word in the term means. A fossil is the remains of something that lived long ago. Fuel is a material used to produce energy.

How do these definitions help you understand how coal, oil, and gas were formed?

_____

_____

_____

 1.g. Students know electrical energy can be changed to heat, light, and motion.

189

1. What are two reasons to conserve fossil fuels?

a. _____

_____

b. _____

_____

2. On the circle graph, circle each number that stands for the amount of electricity that comes from burning a fossil fuel.

3. How does the amount of electricity that comes from burning fossil fuels compare with the amount that comes from other energy sources?

_____

_____

I Wonder . . . What would happen to the environment if more electricity were made from wind and solar power?

_____

_____

_____

190

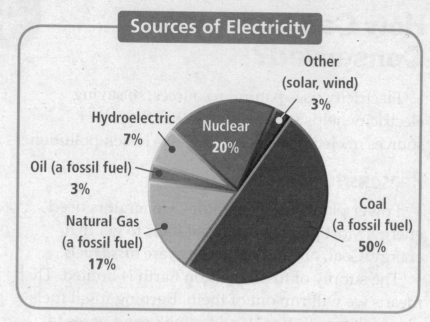

Sources of Electricity

Other (solar, wind) 3%

Hydroelectric 7%

Nuclear 20%

Oil (a fossil fuel) 3%

Natural Gas (a fossil fuel) 17%

Coal (a fossil fuel) 50%

The United States gets most of its electricity by burning fossil fuels, including oil, natural gas, and coal.

Alternate Energy Sources

We can use more than fossil fuels to make energy. One way is with hydroelectric (HY droh ee LEHK trihk) power. Hydroelectric power plants use moving water to run generators. This power also causes pollution.

Wind power is being used more often. The wind blows giant blades, like the ones on a fan. This creates power for a generator.

Solar energy is energy from the Sun. It can also be used to make electric current. Solar energy does not use magnets. It changes solar energy directly into electrical energy.

What You Can Do

The best way to lessen pollution and save natural resources is to conserve electricity. If you use less electricity, then fewer resources will be needed.

Turn off lights.

Use cold water.

Don't leave the refrigerator door open.

Only run the dishwasher when it is full.

Turn off TVs, radios, and stereos.

MAIN IDEA

What are two ways to get power to generate electric current?

Summary Finding other sources of electrical energy helps to save resources. Using less electricity helps save natural resources. Complete the diagram to show three ways that you can help save electricity.

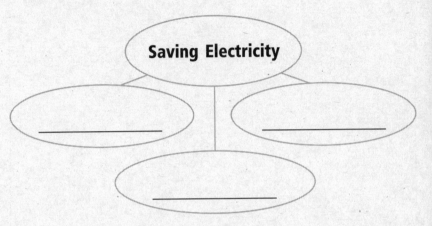

Saving Electricity

Main Idea What are two ways to get power to generate electric current?

_____

_____

_____

_____

Glossary

Choose one of the vocabulary words and draw a picture of it.

Glossary

aurora (uh ROHR uh) A display of lights in the sky caused by particles from the Sun interacting with Earth's magnetic field and atmosphere.

aurora Luces del cielo causadas por partículas procedentes del Sol que interactúan con el campo magnético y la atmósfera terrestre.

compass (KUHM puhs) An instrument that senses magnetic north using a free-moving magnet.

brújula Instrumento que localiza el norte magnético por medio de un imán en movimiento.

electromagnet (ih lehk troh MAG niht) A strong temporary magnet that uses electricity to produce magnetism.

electroimán Imán potente que funciona con electricidad para producir magnetismo.

fossil fuels (faw SIHL fyoolz) Natural fuels such as coal, oil, or natural gas.

combustibles fósiles Combustibles naturales, como el carbón, el petróleo o el gas natural.

generator (JEHN uh ray tuhr) A device that uses magnetism to convert energy of motion into electrical energy.

generador Dispositivo que funciona con magnetismo para convertir la energía cinética en energía eléctrica.

magnet (MAG niht) An object that attracts certain metals.

imán Objeto que atrae ciertos metales.

Glossary

magnetic field (mag NEHT ihk feeld) The space in which the force of a magnet can act.

campo magnético Espacio en el que actúa la fuerza de un imán.

magnetic poles (mag NEHT ihk pohlz) Two areas where the force of a magnet is at its greatest.

polos magnéticos Las dos zonas donde es más potente la fuerza de un imán.

motor (MOH tuhr) A device that changes electrical energy to energy of motion.

motor Dispositivo que convierte la energía eléctrica en energía cinética.

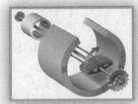

permanent magnet (PUHR mahn uhnt MAG niht) An object that keeps its magnetism for a long time.

imán permanente Un objeto que mantiene su magnetismo durante mucho tiempo.

temporary magnet (TEHM puhr ayr ee MAG niht) An object that loses its magnetism after a short time.

imán temporal Un objeto que mantiene su magnetismo por poco tiempo.

 Visit www.eduplace.com to play puzzles and word games.

Circle the words in this Glossary that are the same in both English and Spanish.

Chapter Review

WHAT DID YOU LEARN?

Vocabulary

❶ Circle the correct answer on the page.

Comprehension

❷ _____

❸ _____

❹ _____

_____

Critical Thinking

❺ _____

_____

_____

_____

Responding

Think About What You Have Read

Vocabulary

❶ An instrument that senses magnetic north is a/an _____.

A) generator

B) compass

C) aurora

D) motor

Comprehension

❷ The two ends of a magnet are called the _____.

❸ The north pole of a magnet will repel _____.

❹ How do a clock and a fan use electricity differently?

Critical Thinking

❺ Which would be more useful for moving heavy iron objects in industry: an electromagnet or a permanent magnet? Explain.

Index

A

Acid rain, 141
Adaptations, 39–45
Agriculture, 88, 93–94
Air, 4–7, 8, 20, 47
Air pollution, 189, 190
Algae, 22, 70
Alluvial fan, 146
Alternate energy sources,
　190–191
Animals
　adaptations of, 39–45
　carnivores, 62
　changes in habitat and, 44–46
　changes people make and,
　　84–87
　of chaparral, 18
　communities and populations
　　of, 11
　competition for resources,
　　47–48
　as consumers, 59–62
　of deserts, 7, 16–17
　extinction of, 46
　food of, 34, 41, 59, 60, 62
　of forests, 6, 10, 12
　of freshwater ecosystems,
　　23–24
　herbivores, 61
　interdependence of, 32–38
　life processes of, 9
　needs of, 8, 32–33, 34–36
　of oceans, 20–22
　omnivores, 62
　of the polar regions, 7
　as pollinators, 37
　predators and prey, 41, 43,
　　50–51, 59
　scavengers, 76–78
　seed dispersal by, 38
　of taiga, 19
　of temperate zone, 10
　of tropical rainforest, 14–15
Atoms, 158–160
Attraction, 159, 178, 179, 180,
　185
Auroras, 183

B

Bacteria, 67–68, 79, 80
Bamboo, 45
Battery, 161, 165
Bays, 145
Biodegradable, 88
Birds, 37, 38, 77
Building design, 126

C

California redwood forest, 35
Camouflage, 39, 42
Canopy, 14–15
Carnivores, 58, 62, 77
Cars, 171
Cell, 67
Cementing, 112, 115
Chaparral, 14, 18
Chemicals, 140, 141
Circuit breaker, 166
Cirque, 149, 150
Cleavage, 102, 105, 106, 107–109
Cleavage planes, 105
Closed circuit, 163
Coastal ocean, 21
Color of minerals, 103, 106,
　107–109
Community, 8, 11
Compass, 182
Competition, 47–51, 62

Composting, 76, 82–83, 90
Conductor, 161, 162, 165
Conservation, 88–95, 189, 191
Consumers, 32, 34, 58–66
 carnivores, 62, 63
 decomposers, 76, 79–83
 in food chain, 61–66, 69–70
 in food webs, 64–66
 herbivores, 61, 63
 omnivores, 62–63
 predators, 41, 43, 48, 50–51,
  59–60
 scavengers, 76–78
Continents, 110
Coral reef, 20, 21
Core of the Earth, 110
Cover crops, 94
Creep, 122, 123
Crop rotation, 94
Crust of Earth, 110, 111, 122–127,
 131
Crystals, 111

D

Dams, 85, 147
Decay, 76, 79–83
Decomposers, 76, 79–83
Delta, 146

Deposition, 144, 146, 149, 152
Desert, 7, 14, 16–17, 40
Discharge, 160

E

Earth
 deposition on, 144–147, 149
 earthquakes on, 122–127, 131
 erosion on, 142–143, 148, 151
 landslides, 131–134
 layers of, 110
 as a magnet, 181–183
 rapid changes in, 122–134
 rocks of crust of, 110, 111–115
 slow changes in, 114–115,
  140–152
 volcanoes, 128–130
 weathering, 112, 115, 140, 143,
  151
Earthquakes, 122–127, 131
Ecosystems, 88
 adaptations to, 39–45
 in balance, 50–51
 California redwood forest, 35
 chaparral, 14, 18
 communities and populations
  of, 10
 coral reef, 20, 21

decomposers in, 79–83
deserts, 7, 14, 17, 40
energy pyramid in, 63
food chains in, 61–66
food webs in, 64–66
forests, 5–6, 10, 12, 40
fresh water, 23–24, 87
interdependence of organisms
 of, 32–38
living things reactions to, 9
nonliving things of, 4–7
of oceans, 20–22
peoples' effects on, 84–87
polar areas, 5, 7
pollution of, 86–87
preservation of, 88–95
rainforest, 14
recycling nutrients in, 76, 80–83
scavengers in, 76–78, 83
taiga, 14, 19
in a terrarium, 13
tundra, 40
Ecotourism, 88, 92
Electric charge, 158–160
 conductors and insulators, 162
 electric circuits, 162, 163–166
 electric current, 162
 static electricity, 160, 161
 switches, 163

Electric circuits, 161, 163–166

Electric current, 161, 169–170, 184, 185

Electricity

change of form, 161, 168–171, 186

conductors and insulators, 162

conservation of, 189, 191

cost of, 188

electric circuits, 161, 163–166

electric current, 161, 169–170, 184, 185

electromagnets and, 184–187

generation of, 187–191

motors and, 186

resistance and, 169–170

safety, 167

static electricity, 160, 161

switches, 163

unit of measure, 161

uses for, 168–171

Electromagnets, 184–187

Energy, 8

change of form, 161, 168–171

conservation of, 189

cost of electricity, 188

cycle of in ecosystems, 58–63

electric charge, 158–160

electric current, 161–163, 169–170

from food, 8, 58–59, 63

food chains and, 61–66, 69–70

generation of electricity, 187, 189–190

living things' need of, 8, 9

sources of, 58, 60, 190

Energy pyramid, 63

Environment, 11

adaptations to, 39–45

peoples' effects on, 84–87

preservation of, 88–95

Epicenter, 122, 126

Erosion, 142–143, 148, 151

Erratic, 149, 150

Extinction, 39, 46

F

Facets, 105

Falcons, 44

Faults, 122, 126

Fertilizers, 93, 94

Fires, 18, 131

Floodplain, 146

Floods, 146

Focus, 122, 125

Food

algae as, 22

of carnivores, 77

competition for, 47

of decomposers, 79–83

food web, 77–78

made by microorganisms, 67, 70

made by plants, 32, 58, 60, 61

of predators, 43, 48, 50–51, 77

producers and consumers, 34

of scavengers, 76–78

Food chains, 61–66, 69–70

Food webs, 64–66, 70, 76–78, 79–83

Forest floor, 14–15

Forests, 5–6, 10, 12

adaptations to, 40

California redwood forest, 35

clearing of, 84–85

preservation of, 91–92, 95

rainforests, 14–15, 40, 91–92

Fossil fuels, 189

Freshwater ecosystems, 23–24

Fungi, 79, 80

Fuse, 166

G

Gemstones, 105

Generators, 184, 187, 189–190

Glaciers, 143, 144, 148–150, 152
Green agriculture, 88, 93–94
Growth, 9

H

Habitat, 39
  adaptations to, 39–45
  desert, 40
  forests, 40
  rainforest, 40
  tundra, 40
Hardness, 102, 104, 106–109
Hazardous waste, 84, 87
Headlands, 145
Heart, 167
Heat, 161, 168, 169, 188
Herbivores, 58, 61
Hibernate, 39, 43
Humans, 84–87, 88, 147, 167
Hybrid cars, 171
Hydroelectric power, 190

I

Ice, 140, 143, 148–150
Igneous rock, 110, 111, 115
Inner core of the Earth, 110
Insects, 37

Insulator, 161
Interdependence, 32–38
Iron, 178, 184–185

K

Kelp forests, 21

L

Lakes, 24, 150
Landfills, 89–90, 95
Landslides, 131–134
Lava, 128–130
Leaves, 58
Life processes, 9
Light
  converting electricity to, 161,
    170
  as nonliving thing in
    ecosystems, 4–7
  in oceans, 20
  plants' need of, 6, 49
  in tropical rainforest, 14–15
Like charges, 158–159, 179
Litter, 84, 86, 87
Living things, 8
  adaptations of, 39–45
  changes in habitat and, 44–46

changes people make and,
    84–87
  of chaparral, 18
  communities and populations
    of, 11
  competition for resources,
    48–51
  consumers, 58–66
  decomposers, 76, 79–83
  of deserts, 17
  in ecosystems, 4–7
  extinction of, 46
  food chain and, 61–66
  of the forest, 6, 10, 12
  of freshwater ecosystems,
    23–24
  interdependence of, 32–38
  life processes of, 9
  microorganisms, 67–70
  needs of, 8, 13–14, 58
  of oceans, 20–22
  predators and prey, 41
  producers, 58–67
  scavengers, 76–78
  species of, 39
  of taiga, 19
  of temperate zone, 10
  of tropical rainforest, 14–15
Luster, 102, 106, 107–109

M

Magma, 128–130
Magnetic field, 178, 180, 181, 183
Magnetic materials, 108
Magnetic poles, 178, 179, 181
Magnets, 178–180
  auroras and, 183
  compasses and, 182
  Earth as magnet, 181–183
  electromagnets, 184–187
  generators and, 187–190
  magnetic field, 180, 181, 183
  motors and, 186
  poles of, 179, 181
  temporary and permanent, 178, 179, 184, 186, 187
Magnitude of earthquakes, 126
Mantle of Earth, 110
Metallic minerals, 107–109
Metamorphic rock, 110, 113, 114–115
Microorganisms, 67–70
Mimicry, 39, 42
Minerals, 106
  cleavage of, 105, 106, 107–108
  color and streak of, 103, 106, 107–109
  description of, 102, 106
  hardness of, 104, 106, 107–109
  identification of, 107–109
  luster of, 102, 106, 107–109
  metallic and nonmetallic, 107–109
  in rocks, 110
Mohs scale, 104
Mold, 79
Moose, 50–51, 77
Moraine, 149, 150
Motion, 161, 171, 186, 187
Motors, 171, 186
Mountains, 126, 150
Mount St. Helens, 130, 131
Mudslides, 131

N

Negative charge, 158–160
Neutral particles, 158, 159
Nonliving things
  of chaparral, 18
  of deserts, 7, 16–17
  in ecosystems, 4–7, 8, 13
  of forests, 5–6, 12, 14–15
  of freshwater ecosystems, 23–24
  minerals, 102–109
  in oceans, 20–22
  of polar areas, 5, 7
  of taiga, 19
  of the temperate zone, 10
  in terrariums, 13
Nonmetallic minerals, 107
Nuclear power plants, 187
Nutrients, 49
  living things' need of, 8, 9
  recycling of in ecosystems, 76, 80–83
  in soils, 94

O

Oceans, 20–22
  changes to shorelines, 144–145
  floor of, 110
  oil spills in, 87
  plankton in, 69–70
  tsunami and, 125
Oil spills, 87
Omnivores, 62, 78
Open circuit, 163
Open ocean, 22
Organic farming, 94

Organisms. *See* Living things
Outer core of Earth, 110
Oxygen, 8, 22, 70, 91

P

Pandas, 45, 46
Parallel circuits, 161, 164, 166
Particles, electric charge on,
  158–160
Passenger pigeons, 46
People, 84, 147, 167
Permanent magnets, 178, 179,
  184, 186, 187
Photosynthesis, 58, 61, 70
Plankton, 24, 67, 69–70
Plants
  adaptations of, 39–45
  changes people make and,
    84–87
  of chaparral, 18
  communities and populations
    of, 11
  competition for resources, 47,
    49
  of deserts, 7, 17
  fire and, 18

food made by, 34, 58, 60, 61
of forest, 12
of freshwater ecosystems,
  23–24
interdependence of, 32–38
life processes of, 9
needs of, 4, 8, 34–36, 49
of oceans, 20–22
oxygen and, 8
as producers, 58–62
of rainforests, 91–92
rock weathering by roots of,
  140, 141
of taiga, 19
of temperate zone, 10
of tropical rainforest, 14–15
Polar areas, 5
Poles of a magnet, 179, 181
Pollen, 37
Pollinators, 32, 37
Pollutants, 84, 86–87
Pollution, 84, 86–87, 93, 189,
  190, 191
Ponds, 24
Population, 8, 11, 48, 50–51
Positive charge, 158–159
Predators, 39, 41, 43, 48, 50–51,
  59, 63, 77–78

Preservation, 88–95
Prey, 39, 41, 43, 50–51, 59, 63
Producers, 32, 34, 58–66
Properties
  of magnets, 178
  of minerals, 102–109

R

Rain, 16–17, 131
Rainforests, 14–15, 40, 91–92
Reactions to environment, 9
Recycling, 88, 90, 95
Repelling, 159
Reproduction, 8, 9, 37
Repulsion, 179
Resistance, 169–170
Resources, 47–51
Reusing, 90
Richter scale, 126
Rivers, 23, 85, 146–147
River systems, 146
Rock, 110
  cycle of, 114–115
  erosion of, 142–143
  igneous rock, 110, 111, 113
  metamorphic rock, 113

sedimentary rock, 112, 113
  in volcanoes, 128–130
  weathering of, 112, 115,
    140–141, 143, 151
Rock cycle, 114–115
Rockslides, 131, 134
Roots, 49

S

Safety, electrical, 167
Saltwater ecosystems, 20–21
San Andreas Fault, 123
Sand dunes, 152
Scavengers, 76–78, 83
Sediment
  dams and, 85
  deposition of, 144, 146, 152
  erosion of, 151
  sedimentary rock formation
    and, 110, 112, 115
Sedimentary rock, 110, 112, 115
Seed dispersal, 32, 38
Seeds, 18, 32, 37, 38
Seismology, 122, 126
Series circuits, 161, 164
Shade, 5–6, 14–15
Shelter, 8, 14–15, 33, 36

Shorelines, 20
Snow, 131
Soil, 49
  compost and, 81–82
  of deserts, 16–17
  green agriculture and, 93–94
  as nonliving thing in
    ecosystems, 4–7
  plants' need of, 4, 6
Solar energy, 190
Solar wind, 183
Sound, 161, 168
Space to live, 47, 48, 82
Species, 39, 46
Static electricity, 158, 160, 161
Streak, 102, 103, 106
Streams, 23, 146
Sugar, 58
Sun
  auroras and, 183
  energy from, 4–7, 20, 49, 58,
    60, 70, 190
  as nonliving thing in
    ecosystems, 4–7
  in oceans, 20
  photosynthesis and, 49, 58, 61
  rock weathering by, 141
Switches, 163

T

Taiga, 14, 19
Temperate zone, 8, 10
Temperature
  in chaparral, 18
  in deserts, 7, 16
  in polar areas, 5, 7
  in taiga, 19
  of temperate zone, 10
  in tropical rainforest, 14
Temporary magnets, 178, 179,
  184
Terrarium, 13
Trees
  in California redwood forest,
    35
  in forests, 5–6, 10, 12, 14–15
  relationship with ants, 33
  as shelter, 36
  in taiga, 19
Tropical rainforest, 14–15
Tsunami, 122, 125
Tundra, 40

U

Understory, 14–15
Unlike charges, 158–159, 179

V

Valleys, 126, 150
Volcanoes, 128–130, 131

W

Waste
  given off by living things, 9
  landfills and, 89–90
  pollution with, 84, 86, 87
  recycling, reusing, composting,
    90
  zero waste programs, 95
Water, 49
  competition for, 47
  deposition by, 144–147
  in deserts, 16–17
  erosion by, 142–143
  of freshwater ecosystems,
    23–24
  generation of electricity with,
    187, 190
  living things' need of, 6, 8
  as nonliving thing in
    ecosystems, 4–7
  of oceans, 20–21
  pollution of, 86–87, 93

rock weathering by, 140, 141
  shaping the land, 144–147
  in taiga, 19
  in tropical rainforest, 14–15
Watt, 161
Weathering, 112, 115, 140, 143,
  151
Wildfires, 131
Wind
  deposition by, 144, 145, 152
  erosion by, 143
  generation of electricity with,
    187, 190
  as a pollinator, 37
  seed dispersal by, 38
  weathering by, 151
Wolves, 51, 77

Y

Yeast, 67, 68

Z

Zero waste, 95